A VERY SHORT,
FAIRLY INTERESTING AND
REASONABLY CHEAP BOOK ABOUT
STUDYING LEADERSHIP

A VERY SHORT, FAIRLY INTERESTING AND REASONABLY CHEAP BOOK ABOUT STUDYING LEADERSHIP

BRAD JACKSON AND KEN PARRY

Los Angeles | London | New Delhi
Singapore | Washington DC

The title for the 'Very Short, Fairly Interesting and Reasonably Cheap Book about ... Series' was devised by Chris Grey. His book, *A Very Short, Fairly Interesting and Reasonably Cheap Book about Studying Organizations*, was the founding title of this series.

Chris Grey asserts his rights to be recognized as founding editor of the **Very Short, Fairly Interesting and Reasonably Cheap Book about ... Series**

SAGE Publications Ltd
1 Oliver's Yard
55 City Road,
London EC1Y 1SP

SAGE Publications Inc.
2455 Teller Road
Thousand Oaks, California 91320

SAGE Publications India Pvt Ltd
B 1/I 1 Mohan Cooperative Industrial Area
Mathura Road, New Delhi 110 044

SAGE Publications Asia-Pacific Pte Ltd
33 Pekin Street #02-01
Far East Square
Singapore 048763

Library of Congress Control Number: 2007927415

British Library Cataloguing in Publication data

A catalogue record for this book is available
from the British Library

ISBN 978-1-4129-2845-8 (hbk)
ISBN 978-1-4129-2846-5 (pbk)

Typeset by C&M Digitals (P) Ltd., Chennai, India
Printed and bound in Great Britain by Athenaeum Press, Gateshead
Printed on paper from sustainable resources

Contents

About the authors   vi

Acknowledgements   ix

Should you Buy This Book?   1

1 Introduction: Why Studying Leadership Matters   3

2 Leader-centred Perspectives on Leadership   23

3 Follower-centred Perspectives on Leadership   41

4 Cultural Perspectives on Leadership   61

5 Critical Perspectives on Leadership   83

6 Leadership with a Higher Purpose   97

7 Conclusion: Take Your Lead   113

References   131

Appendix: Resources for Studying Leadership   147

Index   151

About the authors

Brad Jackson is the Fletcher Building Education Trust Professor of Leadership at the University of Auckland Business School. He was formerly Director of the Centre for the Study of Leadership and Head of School of the Management School at Victoria University of Wellington in New Zealand. Brad has been a Visiting Associate Professor with the Copenhagen Business School in Denmark and an Associate Professor of Continuing Education at the University of Calgary in Canada.

Jackson's research interests include: strategic and cross-cultural leadership, the management advice industry and qualitative research methodologies. He has taught courses in leadership, organizational behaviour, change management, inter-cultural management, organizational communication, and management learning.

Jackson has spoken to academic and business audiences throughout the world and has published three books – *Management Gurus and Management Fashions*, *The Hero Manager* and *Organisational Behaviour in New Zealand*.

Prior to moving to New Zealand in June 1999, Brad managed the corporate communications department for TransAlta Corporation, a fully integrated energy company. All told he spent over fifteen years in the executive and management development field at the University of Calgary, the Banff Centre for Management, and Mount Royal College. Jackson has a PhD in Management Learning from Lancaster University and has also obtained a MA from the University of British Columbia and a BSc from the University of Bristol, both of which are in Geography.

Ken Parry is a Professor of Management at Griffith Business School, specializing in leadership studies. Prior to this, between 1998 and 2003, he was the Foundation Director of the Centre for the Study of Leadership. The centre was a joint venture between Victoria University and the New Zealand College of Management, a private industry training provider. Before taking up his first academic post at the University of Southern Queensland, Ken spent nine years in the private sector as an inventory manager in the manufacturing industry.

Ken is the editor of the *Journal of Management & Organization* and is a Fellow of the Australian Institute of Management and the Australian Human Resources Institute. He teaches courses in leadership, organizational change, organizational behaviour and human resource management.

His research interests include leadership, organizational change, chief executive-board leadership and grounded theory research. Ken has either written or edited six books – *Grounding Leadership Theory and Research*, *The Hero Manager*, *Leadership in the Antipodes*, *Human Resource Management*, *Transformational Leadership* and *Leadership Research and Practice*.

Ken has a PhD from Monash University, a Master of Business from the University of Southern Queensland and a BA from the University of Queensland.

Acknowledgements

We'd like first and foremost to acknowledge Christopher Grey who came up with the idea for this type of book with his own *A Very Short, Fairly Interesting and Reasonably Cheap Book About Studying Organizations* (Grey, 2005). We'd like to thank Sage for believing in and supporting that book and for coming up with the distinctive Adrian Mole-like cover which this book cover echoes. When we first saw Chris' book we thought 'Now, why didn't we write that book?'. It was clever, fresh, edgy and actually quite funny and it created a valuable new niche for organization and management studies books which have traditionally been quite staid and generally dull. Several months later we were delighted when Kiren Shoman from Sage invited us to write a sequel to this book which would focus its attention on studying leadership. Anne Summers and Katherine Haw have also assisted the publication of this book with admirable aplomb and professionalism.

The majority of the ideas and much of the material for this book has been road-tested with postgraduate and undergraduate, MBA and executive programme students in Australia, Canada, Denmark, New Zealand and the United Kingdom. The enthusiasm with which these students have participated in our courses and the feedback they provided has been very helpful in shaping the book's content and style – we have kept them first and foremost in our minds while writing this book.

In researching this book we would especially like to acknowledge the efforts of Dale Pfeifer, Research Fellow for the Centre of the Study of Leadership (CSL) at Victoria University of Wellington who helped us formulate the scope and intent of the book and dug out a lot of key sources for the book, as well as providing thoughtful feedback. The commitment to leadership that she and her colleague, Pam Blakemore, evinces is an inspiration to us. Though now both former directors of the CSL, we are pleased to see the Centre endure and thrive.

We are also indebted to the institutions in which we have taken up chairs in leadership. Ken joined Griffith University in April 2003 and would like to acknowledge his colleagues Paul Rowland, Michael Powell, Ray Weekes, Ashley Goldsworthy, Brian Finn and Soheil Ebedian. Ken is also grateful for the generosity of spirit and visionary thinking of members of the New Zealand College of Management, including Mike Louden, George Hickton, Lyn Provost and David Moloney.

In the middle of writing this book Brad took up the post of Fletcher Building Education Trust Professor of Leadership at the University of Auckland Business School. He would like to thank all of his colleagues in the Department of Management and Employment Relations as well as Excelerator: The New Zealand Leadership Institute for making him so welcome, especially Mark Bentley, Judy Bonny, Giles Burch, Brigid Carroll, Liliana Erakovic, Annick Janson, Darl Kolb, Jolene Francouer, Lester Levy, Barry Spicer, Margaret Tibbles, Mattie Wall, Marie Wilson and Rachel Wolfgram.

We have been very fortunate to have either worked or interacted with some of the best minds in the leadership studies business. We would particularly like to acknowledge the influence of Nancy Adler, Bruce Avolio, Bernie Bass, Alan Bryman, John Burgoyne, Timothy Clark, David Collinson, Patrick Dawson, Deanne Den Hartog, Peter Dorfman, Graham Elkin, Michael Elmes, Keith Grint, David Grant, Eric Guthey, Kerr Inkson, Janet Holmes, Steve Kempster, Alan Lind, Ngatata Love, Meredith Marra, Pushkala Prasad, Arja Ropo, Majken Schulz, Amanda Sinclair, Dennis Tourish and Mary Uhl-Bien.

Finally, we'd like to thank our families for letting us write a second book together and for allowing us to slip away on weekends to get this book written. Brad has learned more about leadership from his wife Jacquie and two children, Devan and Colin, than he is generally willing to admit. Ken would like to say a heartfelt thanks to his wife Margie, and sons Hamish and Jonathan.

Should you Buy This Book?

In common with the first and very original book in this series, Christopher Grey's *A Very Short, Fairly Interesting and Reasonably Cheap Book About Studying Organizations* (Grey, 2005), this book is designed mainly for university students who are studying leadership, or perhaps contemplating studying leadership as part of a senior undergraduate or a postgraduate course. You may, in fact, be on the verge of starting a project, dissertation or thesis on leadership and want to get a handle on the various ways that you might go about doing this.

It is not a textbook. As the title infers it is much shorter, hopefully more interesting and considerably cheaper than a text – and it is a lot more portable. Indeed we have written this book so that it can be comfortably read on a four-hour plane or train ride with time built in for dinner – think of it as middle-brow 'in-flight edutainment'. The downside is that it is a lot less colourful than a textbook and there are no pictures. We have tried to make up for this lack of visual content with our lucid prose, graphic imagery and biting wit, but we'll let you be the judge of that.

This book may also be of interest to those who are not currently engaged in a formal programme of study but have always had an interest in leadership. Understandably, you may be getting more than a little tired and somewhat disenchanted with the same old ghost-written 'I did it my way' biographies of business leaders or the 'Eleven leadership secrets' book-sized business cards written by faceless consultants. In fact, you may be looking for something with a little more intellectual grunt but aren't quite ready yet to dive into the academic abyss. We hope, of course, that after reading this book, you'll promptly march down to your nearest seat of learning and sign up for a formal programme to find others who have already decided to make that fateful leap. But we would say that, wouldn't we?

Finally, the book may also be of interest to our academic colleagues who have heard a lot about this thing called leadership recently, and are curious to find out what all the fuss is about and potentially how they might add to this fuss. We spend a lot of time trying to convince our colleagues from other disciplines such as anthropology, classics, history and political science that leadership research is (a) a legitimate academic pursuit and (b) what they might already be doing themselves but are not explicitly aware of this. To you we say: 'the more the merrier'.

If you do buy this book and would like to enquire further, take issue or even praise this book you can e-mail either Brad at b.jackson@auckland.ac.nz or Ken at k.parry@griffith.edu.au. We look forward to hearing from you.

Introduction: Why Studying Leadership Matters

'I believe that we are more likely to secure responsible leadership in the future if we can demystify its constituent processes. In that sense, enhanced knowledge about leadership may go hand-in-hand with more morally desirable forms of leadership'.

Howard Gardner, Leading Minds (1995)

▓▓▓▓ on studying leadership

The *Concise Oxford Dictionary* defines 'study' variously as 'a thing to be secured by pains or attention', 'devotion of time and thought to acquiring information especially from books', 'be on the watch, try constantly to manage', 'a thing that deserves to be investigated' and the definition we particularly enjoy, 'a fit of musing, reverie' – something that we hope this book might invoke for you. There are broadly five ways that one can go about studying leadership. You can actually attempt to lead, you can observe leadership in action, you can talk about leadership, you can read about it and you can write about it.

Given that we are both professors, it won't surprise anyone to learn that we find it easiest to *talk* about leadership. After all, we do this all the time in our lectures, seminars and workshops. We are greatly assisted in this regard by the fact that everyone has a fundamental interest in leaders and leadership. It's certainly true that everybody we have ever talked with has developed some kind of opinion on what constitutes good and bad leadership. Whether it's teenagers' views on the adequacy of their parents' or teachers' leadership skills or a colleague questioning the wisdom of promoting someone at work or the election of a new political leader, leadership tends to be something that is high on a lot of people's agendas – and invariably it's a powerful way of dividing people into those who support a particular leader and those who do not. The most authoritative sources regarding matters of global as well as local leadership are, of course, taxi drivers. They should be consulted at every opportunity.

As we will see there is no shortage of opportunities to read about leadership. Leadership books continue to be a mainstay of publishers' catalogues. Amazon.com has more than 5,000 non-fiction books with the word 'leadership' in their title. Where we hope we can help rather than hinder by adding one more title to this list, is to guide you through the maze and encourage you to go beyond the conventional mainstream popular fare which dominates the shelves of high street book stores. People read leadership books for a number of reasons: to be inspired by others who have faced and overcome even greater odds than we are facing; to be reassured that we are not doing so badly after all; or simply to be entertained. We want to encourage you to select leadership books because they challenge, unearth, expand and perhaps even subvert your assumptions about leadership, and what it is to lead and to follow.

Reading about leadership should not be confined to books; the newspaper is a prime source of leadership stories. The next time you pick up your newspaper try counting how many times the term 'leader' or 'leadership' appears in it. Most students recognize that these terms will show up quite frequently in the business and politics sections but are surprised to learn how often leaders and leadership crop up in the sports and entertainment sections. Of course, the section in which these terms are most frequently mentioned is the career opportunities section – yet another reason to become interested in studying leadership.

Another great source for leadership stories can be found at the movies. While we do not wish to undermine any welcome relief from the worries of the world that you may derive from going to the movies, we do hope that, like us, you will never be able to watch a movie again without thinking that it is a movie about leadership. From *Alien* to *Zorro* all you will see are leadership lessons; the fun is well and truly over! To get you started, we've provided you with our list of all-time favourite leadership movies in the Appendix.

Writing about leadership is more challenging. We find that the 'publish or perish' stick used in concert with the 'fame and fortune' carrot can prove to be surprisingly strong motivators for academics. Perhaps the relief of getting assignments done and out of the way, coupled with the affirming allure of superior grades, may well do it for you. Whatever it takes it is very important to find time to write as there is something very special about the writing process. Its solitary, reflective and permanent nature requires a much stronger commitment to say what you really think, compared to everyday conversation or discourse. The off-the-cuff remark or observation that seemed so appropriate and pithy at the time reveals itself to be less so once vulnerably placed on the written page. However, when you do finally work an argument through to its logical conclusion, you can reach a level of contentment that is hard to match.

We tend to value our leaders primarily for their abilities as orators. However, many of them use the written word through the medium of their diaries and memoirs to make sense of and to work through the dilemmas, their doubts and their frustrations associated with their leadership positions. Nelson Mandela's magnificent autobiographical bestseller, *Long Walk to Freedom*, is an exemplar of this form of leadership communication. It's not surprising, then, that these documents attract so much interest when they are made public. People are naturally curious to see what lurks behind the front-stage of the theatre of leadership. Unfortunately, they can occasionally be disappointed as demonstrated in Bill Clinton's verbose and generally unrevealing autobiography, *My Life*.

Seeing leadership, if done superficially, is not difficult at all. It's something we all do day in and day out. To quote a well-worn epithet, leadership is like beauty – it is difficult to describe, but we certainly know it when we experience it. Most of the time we rely on the media to guide us, and make it easy for us to understand and judge. Whether it's a beleaguered politician, the coach of a sports team on a losing streak or a business tycoon embroiled in a business scandal, the media can be especially persuasive about what constitutes good and bad leadership and how it needs to be addressed. Usually they recommend instant removal. However, we believe it is important to want to see leadership though our own eyes. Having the discipline to observe leadership properly requires time, patience, imagination and the willingness constantly to question what one is observing and to look for new and perhaps disconfirming evidence. Most importantly, one needs to look beyond the obvious, take a contrary view and, occasionally, be willing to become unpopular with one's views. In this book we want to develop and foster a multidimensional, broader and even empathetic view of leaders and leadership.

Anyone who has attempted to lead will understand that the act of leadership is considerably more challenging than talking, reading, writing or seeing leadership all put together. There's no doubt that one can learn the most about leadership from actually trying to lead. That has certainly been the case for us in our efforts to lead. It is an inconvenient irony that there is an inverse relationship between the ease and comfort in doing something and the quantity and quality of learning that is generated by it. This irony is further highlighted by the fact that we can often learn the most from situations in which we have failed to lead. Indeed another leadership book was recently published entitled *Firing*

Back: How Great Leaders Rebound After Career Disasters by Jeffrey Sonnenfeld and Andrew Ward. Everybody loves to hear about a comeback story, just don't make a habit of it.

Of course, we can all think of some leaders with whom we have worked who, in common with the infamous David Brent character from TV's *The Office*, appear to be incapable of learning anything from their efforts at leading or from their followers. Thankfully, most leaders we work with are keen to learn and improve their abilities as a leader. The experience of leading seems to sharpen their desire to learn and to change.

In light of the power and importance of experience, the idea of merely studying leadership might seem somewhat passive, evasive and even frivolous. In our roles as directors of a Centre for the Study of Leadership we were often quizzed about the desirability of having such a passive and weak term as 'study' associated with the Centre. Wouldn't it be more marketable to rename it the 'Centre for Leadership' or more simply the 'Leadership Centre'? We held firm to the word 'study' because we believe that there has perhaps been too much emphasis placed upon 'just doing' leadership and not enough, as Howard Gardner's opening quotation signals, on 'demystifying its constituent processes'. We ardently believe that, in order to create the morally responsible forms of leadership that many of us crave, it is vital not only for leaders to demystify these processes but also for followers to do so as we are the people who will guide and influence the leaders.

When we talk about 'studying' leadership we are thinking of all five of these activities: doing, seeing, talking, reading and writing. We not only need to learn to become better at doing all five of these activities but, most significantly, it is critical for us to learn how to better link and integrate these activities into a cohesive philosophical whole. So that what we read influences what we see about leadership, what we talk about helps us to write about leadership which, in turn, helps us to do better leadership. This is by no means a linear process. In fact, you could easily reverse the sequence described above or use various combinations and the process would be equally valid. Though the primary task of this book is to help you learn more about leadership by reading about it, it is our hope that the process of reading about leadership will duly impact on and shape what and how you choose to see, talk, write and do leadership.

where we are coming from

While biographies of pre-eminent leaders will often reveal a desire to lead early on in the life of the leader that has invariably been engendered by a major setback or by an inspirational figure or a general expectation placed upon them, it's fair to admit that nobody consciously sets out to study leadership. For reasons that we have yet to grasp, society places a greater premium on actually being a leader (assuming one doesn't fail or, more significantly, appear to fail) rather than on its citizens who make their living out of studying leadership. We suggest a variation of George Bernard Shaw's well-worn maxim about those that can't do, teach might be particularly instructive here. However, we hope that you – fellow student of leadership – wouldn't have it any other way.

Most leadership scholars we are familiar with have come to leadership research in a somewhat indirect and roundabout way. This has begun to change with the advent of postgraduate and, increasingly, undergraduate programmes that are explicitly devoted to studying leadership. But this is only a recent development. Most leadership researchers tend to have backgrounds either in psychology (originally from social psychology but more recently from organizational psychology), or they have their roots in sociology, history or political science. Most also come to leadership studies having done something else beyond academe – frequently consulting, teaching, training or project management – and have been drawn into academia because of a profound curiosity they have developed about leadership processes and, almost invariably, a vague desire to help make the world a better place. Leadership scholars tend to be the token dreamers, the chronic optimists and the hopeless romantics that you will find huddled together in small clusters at most business schools. We are no exception to this pattern.

Brad developed his original interest in leadership dynamics for sound practical reasons. As a son of a soldier having to change schools and neighbourhoods on a regular basis, he developed a chameleon-like ability to fit into groups quickly and with minimal fuss. The ability to score a goal during the initial playtime was a particularly effective means of establishing credibility. The other important means for fitting in was to quickly read the prevailing leadership dynamics within the various sub-groups, cliques or gangs, and ensure that one quickly got onside with the good leaders and offside with the bad leaders. This came into sharper focus when he attended military boarding school, where he contended with a dual civilian and military hierarchy as well as the critical informal network that was constantly being negotiated, challenged and reinforced by the boys. It was only later as he moved from a background in geography into the executive and management development field in Canada that he became exposed to some first-rate leadership teachers, as well as legions of middle and senior managers craving enlightenment about the mysterious secrets of leadership. Looking to management gurus for the answer led Brad to explore through his doctoral thesis the peculiarly evangelical brand of charismatic leadership that these gurus wielded to such impressive effect over millions of managers throughout the world, persuading them to take on the latest management fashion that they were promulgating. While he has failed to cash in on the lessons learned from studying the modus operandi of gurus, he has finally found his true cause in life as New Zealand's first professor of leadership. This role he relishes because he is paid to see, talk, read, write and do leadership every day of the year in a country that contains so many leadership lessons.

We believe that leadership is a fundamentally important human experience that can have a very significant bearing on the conduct and the quality of our everyday lives. We say this, not because we have the scientific evidence to back this up. In fact, hard evidence about the impact of leadership is surprisingly and tantalizingly hard to find. We say this because through our own direct experience working in a range of organizations, participating in a number of community and public groups and networks, we have been constantly impressed by the influence that a leader or groups of leaders can have, when they engage with followers to create this special thing called leadership. In fact, it can be mildly addictive. When it is good, it is very good; when it is bad, it is very bad indeed. Moreover, we find ourselves being constantly amazed at the variety and the complexity of the forms that leadership can take wherever we have cared to look for it. In truth, it is this never-ending fascination that keeps us going in our pursuit of studying leadership.

We mention our backgrounds and experiences with leadership because we want to encourage you to think about where your interest in leadership has come from and to consider how your own background and experiences have served to shape your interests and beliefs about leadership. Bruce Avolio describes this as your 'life stream' which, simply defined, 'represents events you accumulate from birth to the present that shape how you choose to influence others and yourself' (2005: 11). You have already developed a fairly sophisticated philosophy of leadership, which is dubbed your 'implicit leadership theory' (Schyns and Meindl, 2005), whether you are explicitly aware of it or not. You have some clear convictions about what you think constitutes the right and the wrong way to lead someone or to be led by someone.

What we hope is that, through the formal and informal study of leadership, you will not only be exposed to other philosophies of leadership by individuals who have devoted their intellectual lives to clarifying, challenging and deepening their philosophies of leadership but, as a result, you will have cause to question and deepen your own philosophy of leadership. This will not only stand you in good stead as a leadership researcher, but also as a leader and as a follower.

▰▰▰ why it is a good time to be studying leadership

As we said at the outset, this book is aimed at those who are either studying leadership or are considering the possibility of doing so. Being passionately committed to studying leadership, we would of course argue that any time is a good time to be studying leadership. However, we would not be stepping out of line by suggesting that there has never been such a good time to study leadership for the following reasons.

To begin with there has never been so much interest in the field. Leadership is widely seen as both the problem and solution to all manner of contemporary issues: from ending world poverty to addressing global warming; from turning around ailing corporations to regenerating local communities; from reviving schools to creating scientific breakthroughs. The hunger and quest for leadership knowledge appears to be insatiable. Typing into the Google search engine on January 15, 2007 we noted more than 257,000,000 entries when we typed in the word 'leader' and more than 168,000,000 entries for the word 'leadership'.

The distinctive feature of leadership is that it would appear that the more we learn about leadership, the more we realize we have to and want to learn. This might go some way toward explaining the dramatic growth of the leadership development field into a multibillion-dollar global industry; an estimated $36 to $60 billion US dollars are expended annually on management and leadership development throughout the world (Burgoyne, 2004). Surprisingly, little of the money that is invested has been invested in evaluating the impact of this investment. There appears to be blind faith in the efficacy of leadership development. In accounting for this faith, John Storey (2004) has pointed to four different types of explanations which probably all have some salience. The conventional explanation points to the increased complexity and rapid pace of contemporary society which demands higher and more creative levels of leadership. The institutional explanation emphasizes the pressure that is exerted on individuals and organizations to emulate others in order to maintain one's credibility. If everyone is doing leadership development, we had better do it too. The sociological explanation highlights the role that leadership can play in legitimizing the authority, power and privilege of elites. It provides a socially acceptable means of justifying the status quo. Finally, the strategic advantage explanation argues that leadership is an intangible asset that must be cultivated in order to gain a rare and valuable source of competitive advantage.

Given the spectacular growth in interest in leadership, it is not surprising to learn that leadership is also beginning to appear on the radar screens of government funders most notably in Europe and Asia. Traditionally in North America, private and philanthropic sources have provided the bulk of funding for leadership research. Consequently, we have witnessed the mushrooming of leadership institutes and research centres throughout the world, many of which are university-affiliated. Perhaps the best known of these are the Gallup Leadership Institute based at the University of Nebraska, Harvard University's Center for Public Leadership, and the Centre for Excellence in Leadership located at Lancaster University. These and others are listed in the Appendix. Leadership centres and institutes tend to have a twofold focus. The stated purpose of Excelerator: The New Zealand Leadership Institute is typical in this regard: 'To enhance the understanding of leadership in New Zealand and take action to ensure the country has talented and skilled leaders who will develop, guide and advance our organisations and communities.'

In addition to these research institutes, universities, particularly those in North America, are beginning to invest heavily in the provision of leadership development opportunities for students in the form of extracurricular activities, such as in-service programmes while they are pursuing either undergraduate and postgraduate degrees. In some universities, for example the Jepson School of Leadership Studies based in Richmond, Virginia, degrees in leadership are offered both at Bachelor and Master levels. These programmes aim to respond directly to the demands of employees, parents and students who are looking for a competitive edge when they move into the job market.

On the subject of job markets, the more astute readers (we expect all of you to be astute, of course; that's why you have bought this book) will have already recognized that this frenzy of activity will generate – is already generating – significant demand for enthusiastic and well-trained individuals at all levels of seniority who have been well trained in leadership development and research. Perhaps this is where you come in.

the interdisciplinary and applied nature of leadership

Those who work in the leadership research field have always made a point of recognizing its applied and interdisciplinary nature. We research leadership, primarily because we want to make a difference by promoting a better understanding of leadership from which we can help to promote better leadership in practice. While this rationale hangs together in theory, in practice we have probably not been as applied in our effects as we would have liked or perhaps should have been. As John Storey has noted, 'the accumulation of weighty and extensive reports to date tends, in the main, to regurgitate a now familiar thesis – but it is a thesis which remains incomplete, insufficiently tested, inadequately debated and not properly scrutinised' (2004: 6). The bottom line is, there is still plenty of work yet to do – you are most definitely not too late.

Moreover, we have not been as interdisciplinary as we probably should have been in terms of the approaches that we draw upon to conduct leadership research and in terms of the kinds of question that various disciplines might inspire if applied to the study of leadership. Psychology and, to a lesser extent, sociology still tend to dominate the field. There have been, however, some encouraging signs that the leadership field is increasingly branching out and becoming more receptive to a wider range of quantitative as well as qualitative methodologies. The predominant journal in the field and its ultimate arbiter, *The Leadership Quarterly*, has noticeably expanded its agenda to encompass articles with disciplinary and methodological perspectives that would have had only a slim chance of being published in earlier years.

Another bottom line for you then is, even if you feel your disciplinary training might not be directly relevant to studying leadership, it may prove to be a real asset in that it helps you see and conceptualize elements of the leadership process. A good example of this would be one of Brad's former doctoral students, Ralph Bathurst, who drew on his training and experience as a musician (a violist to be precise) to create in his thesis what he described as an 'aesthetic ethnography' aimed at comprehending the 'music of organizations' which he applied to an empirical study of a symphony orchestra to revealing effect.

Leadership is beginning to attract established researchers who may have traditionally eschewed leadership research, either because they were philosophically uneasy about the idea of privileging leaders over followers or because of the field's predominantly functional and positivistic orientation. The arrival in 2005 of a new European-based journal, *Leadership*, is providing an alternative outlet for research with its stated aims of stimulating interest in new methods and theories of leadership; encouraging interdisciplinary, diverse and critical analyses of leadership processes; and providing an international forum for leadership research.

The father of modern leadership studies, James MacGregor Burns, has noted two striking recent developments in the field of leadership studies. The first is the internationalization of the study of leadership. Noting the blossoming of leadership as a discipline in the mid- and late-twentieth century, he comments that 'theoretical work and practical application in non-American contexts will inevitably move leadership theory away from its overly American emphases and bias toward a more international perspective' (2005: 11). The second major development that Burns points to is the role of leadership research as an interdisciplinary endeavour that invigorates related disciplines. Obviously, leadership theory draws heavily from established disciplines but it can also vitalize those disciplines. Burns notes, however,

> 'leadership, in common parlance, is a 'good'. When people call for leadership, or deplore the lack of leadership, they see it not as a needed spur to human progress but, as in itself, a moral and ethical entity and a necessary gauge of action. Leadership, in short, becomes an activity as well as an academic enterprise'. (Burns, 2005: 12)

Leadership scholars are not only growing in number but they are also starting to get better organized (something you would reasonably expect them to do well, given their subject matter). The International Leadership Association (ILA) was formed in 1999 as a means to strengthen ties and share ideas and resources among those who work in leadership studies. In February 2007 it had 628 individual members and 390 institutional members from 33 different countries. In the past three years, the Academy of Management (AOM) has created a Network of Leadership Scholars which brings together several hundred leadership academics who are primarily based in universities. It is remarkable that 200 of the 2,000 papers presented at the annual meeting had 'leadership' in their title. At the end of 2007, Warwick Business School in the UK played host to the sixth International Conference on Studying Leadership – a conference that regularly attracts researchers not only from the UK but from throughout the world.

the problem with leadership

You've had the good news. Now here's the not-so-good news. Leadership is a phenomenon that everyone has an opinion on but few seem to agree exactly on what it really is. Bernard Bass (1990) has famously observed that 'there are almost as many different definitions of leadership as there are persons who have attempted to define it'. From his exhaustive survey of leadership definitions through the twentieth century Joseph Rost concludes, with more than a hint of lament, that a major problem with leadership studies as an academic discipline and with the people who do leadership, is that 'neither the scholars nor the practitioners have been able to define leadership with precision, accuracy, and conciseness so that people are able to label it correctly when they see it happening or when they engage in it.' (1993: 6). We will exemplify what he means with two definitions.

At one end of the continuum of leadership definitions we have the workmanlike but eminently robust definition offered by Stogdill (1974) that conceives of leadership as 'the process of influencing the activities of an organized group in its efforts toward goal setting and goal achievement'. There are three key components of this definition that are worth emphasizing: it is an interpersonal process between one person and a group; you cannot have 'leaders' without 'followers'; and the criterion for effective leadership is goal achievement. If there is no commonly agreed upon and generally understood goal, if it is basically a group of people doing various tasks in an independent fashion, then it is not leadership. At the other end of the continuum, we have the considerably more expansive and flamboyant view of leadership promulgated by Tom Peters and Nancy Austin in their book, *A Passion for Excellence* (1985):

> Leadership means vision, cheerleading, enthusiasm, love, trust, verve, passion, obsession, consistency, the use of symbols, paying attention as illustrated by the content of one's calendar, out-and-out drama (and the management thereof), creating heroes at all levels, coaching, effectively wandering around, and numerous other things ... Leadership must be present at all levels in the organisation. It depends on a million little things done with obsession, consistency and care, but all of those million little things add up to nothing if the trust, vision and basic belief are not there.

You couldn't find two more totally different definitions. Yet from our experience they both point to and illuminate something significant with respect to the experience of leadership. One is more precise and functional, the other is more emotive and suggestive.

Keith Grint in his book *Leadership: Limits and Possibilities* (Grint, 2005) suggests that leadership has traditionally been understood in four quite different ways: Leadership as Person: is it WHO 'leaders' are that makes them leaders? Leadership as Results: is it WHAT 'leaders' achieve that makes them leaders? Leadership as Position: is it WHERE 'leaders' operate that makes them leaders? Leadership as Process: is it HOW 'leaders' get things done that makes them leaders?

We can illustrate these four ways of thinking about leadership with a small case study of leadership. For Brad's benefit, let's take the All Blacks rugby team which, in 2006, completed one of its most successful seasons in its 103-year history. We've already taken the leadership as results perspective by virtue of the fact that we've selected a successful team. We're implying that because the team was so successful it must have had not only good but exceptional leadership. We might however, as most people do when assessing leadership, choose to focus on the leadership as person perspective by pointing to the exceptionally high calibre of the players.

If we were to take the leadership as position perspective we would choose to focus on the role of the head coach of the team, Graham Henry, who, along with his coaching team, has been credited with injecting a culture of discipline, resilience and teamwork into the team. Alternatively, we could point to the contributions of Richie McCaw, the captain, who was named the 2006 International Rugby Board's Player of the Year.

Finally, if we were to follow the leadership as process perspective, we might have elected to focus on the new rotational policy that has been introduced by the coaches, by which All Black players have been moved in and out of the team irrespective of their form. Critics have suggested this has devalued the famous black jersey because so many players are now being given caps. Another leadership as process explanation might focus on the symbolic importance of the Haka, the Maori war dance performed prior to the commencement of each game that reputedly strikes fear in the hearts of opposing teams and inspires the All Black players. A controversial new Haka has been introduced by the players aimed at spurring them on for special occasions.

The fact that we look at leadership in these four different ways goes some way towards explaining why we have so much trouble explaining leadership, trying to understand it, teach it and reward it. In Grint's view, each of these ways of thinking about leadership is valid and potentially useful. He, therefore, does not advocate that leadership scholars should attempt, as Joseph Rost has argued, to develop and agree upon one universal definition of leadership. Instead he believes it should remain an 'essentially contested concept' that is constantly being discussed and debated.

The way in which we have organized this book follows this line of thinking by presenting five different perspectives on leadership which we believe bring something quite valuable to the table in response to the challenge laid down by Howard Gardner in this chapter's opening quotation: to demystify 'the constituent processes of leadership'. It is when we find ways to share and pool our understanding of what constitutes good and effective leadership that we have the opportunity to foster and encourage exceptional leadership within a particular context.

While the importance of the role of individual leaders tends to be overestimated, the significance of leadership itself should never be underestimated. Grint (2005) believes we have become overly preoccupied with individuals leaders when, in fact, we should have been focusing more on leadership. As a result he urges us to 'put the *ship* back into leader*ship*'.

Joseph Rost has attempted to systematically formulate the co-production of leadership by leaders and followers with his definition of leadership which he believes is most appropriate to the 'post-industrial world' that many of us are increasingly working within. He defines leadership as 'an influence relationship among leaders and followers who intend real changes that reflect their mutual purposes' (Rost, 1993: 102).

Rost highlights three essential elements that must be present for genuine leadership to take place. First, the relationship should be based on influence that is multidirectional (i.e. it is exerted downwards, upwards, laterally, within and beyond a particular organization) and non-coercive in that it is not achieved through force. Second, there is typically more than one leader and always more than one follower in the relationship. The followers are active partners but, even in the most democratic groups, the relationship is inevitably, usefully and even necessarily unequal. In responding to the 'Burns Paradox' which asks why we need to differentiate between followers and leaders when they are so intertwined, the eminent leadership scholar, James MacGregor Burns observes:

> The key distinctive role of leadership at the outset is that leaders take the initiative. They address their creative insights to potential followers, seize their attention, spark further interaction. The first act is decisive because it breaks up a static situation and establishes a relationship. It is, in every sense, a *creative* act. (2003: 172)

The third element of Rost's definition is that both leaders and followers work together to bring about substantial rather than superficial changes. These changes are driven by a mutual purpose that is forged through a non-coercive influence relationship. This asymmetrical view of leadership, therefore, does not preclude followers from being active co-producers. In fact, it emphasizes the idea that leaders and followers should share responsibility for any consequences that might arise in the execution of the leadership relationship

Think about the leadership relationships that you have been part of. How many of these do you think would pass the demanding standards set by Rost's definition? Looking back on our careers, we have rarely been part of a genuine leadership relationship within the workplace. The nearest we have come to this has been through our involvement in the wider community through volunteer work. This kind of leadership relationship is something that is quite special and memorable. The point is that this definition is probably best thought of as an aspirational rather than a descriptive definition. It's something that we should aim for if we wish to secure a sustainable future for everybody on the planet: the kind of leadership that is required if we are to confront complex and massive scale issues such as global warming, poverty and the control of virulent diseases. Leaders will continue to play an important role in this relationship. We will still need leaders, but they will be different types of leaders.

▬▬▬ the three questions that are asked most about leadership

We are regularly asked by students, friends and journalists alike, three questions about leadership that we think it would be wise to address early on in the proceedings. What we are keen to show in this book is that, while these questions are not unimportant to leadership scholars, there are many other questions that leadership researchers are actively engaged in answering.

▬▬▬ question 1: are leaders born or made?

We are frequently struck by the number of people we come across who believe that leaders are born and not made. Some defend their position by observing that they have always known – and been told by others – that they are 'natural' leaders. Certainly a strong core self-concept is an important trait for leaders to possess unless it verges on arrogance. Others may not believe that they themselves are natural leaders but they can point to a number of people whom they believe are. We are inclined to react critically to this view on two levels. First on an intellectual level, because we want to know what 'natural' means, where it comes from and how it can be distinguished from 'unnatural'. Second, on a more practical level we are concerned that this stance, by definition, is self-defeating because it rules out the possibility that leadership can and should be learned and, thereby, serves to deter people from developing their full potential.

Bruce Avolio has been tackling this question with admirable gusto. He has estimated from extensive longitudinal research conducted on identical twins born in Sweden, that the 'born' side of the leadership development equation accounts for, on average, approximately 30 per cent of leadership effectiveness. The 'made' side of the equation (i.e. what happens to you after birth) accounts for 70 per cent. He concludes that, 'leadership and wisdom are both made, even if both are built on the genetic abilities people are endowed with at birth like cognitive abilities, energy levels, and how attractive we are to others' (2005: 25). The latter quality, attractiveness, is probably more important than any of us would be willing to admit particularly in persuading others that we should be given the opportunity to lead.

With respect to the making of leadership, Bruce has observed that a combination of authoritative parenting and a proclivity towards modest (but not serious) rule breaking are strong predictors of leadership emergence. The next time you think that your parents may have been a little too strict with you, perhaps there were some benefits in this after all, especially if they allowed you to get away with occasionally bending the rules. Similarly, Manfred Kets de Vries argues that the experience we gain in our first five years plays a most profound role in shaping our desire to lead, as well the ways in which we choose to lead. He describes how the parental disharmony between King Philip and Queen Olympias sowed the seeds of the intense ambition of their son, Alexander the Great, to become an all-conquering leader. Alexander was desperate to take over from his father as the rightful king – an ambition that his all-loving mother did little to dissuade him from harbouring (Kets de Vries, 2004).

While this question has some value in stimulating debate and discussion, and occasionally earning a free drink, it doesn't really help us move forward on the real issue: namely, how do we go about developing the next generation of leaders? We have come across plenty of leaders who were apparently 'born' to be leaders (i.e. they had the 'right' genetic mix, background, etc.) but have not assumed leadership roles or failed miserably as leaders because they were either unable or unwilling to learn. We've also come across those who, on the surface, appear to have been born to follow but choose to learn and succeed in leading instead. It ultimately comes down to aspiration, to the desire to lead.

question 2: what makes an effective leader?

We need to distinguish between two different ways of answering this question: 'the common-sense way' and the 'scientific way'. The 'common-sense way' is an inductive approach which attempts to isolate fundamental truths about leadership that are based on direct and indirect experience with successful leaders. The scientific way is a deductive approach that involves developing a theory of how leadership ought to work and then conducting rigorous analytical experiments to test that theory.

Our own common-sense response to this question is that leaders need to possess many qualities but, if we are pressed, we will concede that five are particularly vital in order to promote effective leadership: confidence, integrity, connection, resilience and aspiration. Confidence creates the essential sense of self-worth and self-efficacy that is needed to put oneself forward to lead and to sustain oneself in a leadership role. Integrity helps leaders to be consistent and allows them to be clear about what they stand for and believe in. Connection is the ability to translate those values through a genuine and authentic link with followers – it is much more than communication, which is often the first choice whenever we ask groups to name what they believe to be the most important quality for a leader to possess. To this we would add resilience, the ability to withstand emotional and physiological stress, setbacks and conflict. Leading can be both psychologically and physiologically draining. You shouldn't be surprised to learn, given our comments above, that we place aspiration at the top of our list of qualities that we believe an effective leader must possess. If you do not aspire to change something and you don't have a good reason for changing it, you cannot and should not lead.

The scientific response to this question adds five more traits to this list. In his review of major research programmes that have attempted to identify predictors of leadership effectiveness, Yukl (2002) points to the following prerequisites. First, a high internal locus of control, which means that the leader believes that events in their own lives are determined more by their own actions than by chance or uncontrollable forces. Second, effective leaders also require a high degree of emotional maturity and stability which has been memorably labelled by Goleman (1995) as 'emotional intelligence'. This means that the leader is able to monitor her or his emotional state and be well aware of their strengths and weaknesses. Third, leaders should also have a high socialized power motivation. This means they should derive enjoyment and fulfilment from influencing people and events for the benefit of others not themselves. Fourth, leaders should also have a moderate but not excessively high achievement orientation as they need to be willing to work with others who may be less capable. Finally, effective leaders should have a low need for affiliation which means that being liked should not be a strong motivator. While leaders should not relish making tough and unpopular decisions, they should not shy away from making them.

question 3: what's the difference between leadership and management?

There is considerable debate about the relationship between leadership and management. One school of thought has stressed that management and leadership are two entirely different functions. For example, Zaleznik (1977) has suggested that leaders develop visions and drive changes, while managers monitor progress and solve problems. Put even more succinctly, Bennis and Nanus (1985) argue that 'managers do things right, while leaders do the right thing'.

Kotter (1990) makes the point that not all managers are leaders and, equally, not all leaders are managers. In fact, we can distinguish between those people in organizations who are 'formal leaders', that is, those who are appointed or elected to positions of formal authority, and those who are 'informal leaders'. Yukl (2002) makes a similar distinction between those leaders who draw on 'position power' and those who draw on 'personal power'. Position power is derived from one's legitimate authority and control over resources, rewards, punishments, information and the physical work environment (i.e. who gets the nicest office). Personal power on the other hand is derived from one's expertise and/or friendship, loyalty and general affability (otherwise known as 'referent power'). You may not be cognizant or even comfortable with the notion that one of the reasons that you may choose to attend a university is to build up a number of these power bases – referent power, of course, being the number one concern. The most powerful leaders strive, in true Machiavellian fashion, to build a 'balanced portfolio' of power bases and are constantly seeking to consolidate and increase their power through the gentle art of political manoeuvring.

Peter Drucker, the management guru's guru, believes that effective managers should strive to be both formal and informal leaders within their organizations (Drucker, 1955). Leadership is one of the key tasks of management alongside planning, controlling and organizing. We can personally attest to the wisdom of this argument having worked for individuals who considered themselves to be leaders and would not denigrate themselves by engaging in any form of management activity. They preferred instead to leave the operational details to others, so that these would not cloud their 'big picture' thinking and get in the way of their vital vision-building activities. We, and the organizations they aspired to lead, ultimately found to their cost that the devil lurks in the detail.

While we are naturally delighted that leadership is being held up in such high regard, we are concerned by what has become conventional wisdom regarding the superiority of leadership over management. If you think of the old cowboy movies, we have got to the point in the popular imagination where the lone sheriff with the white hat who courageously defends the town has come to symbolize leadership (i.e. the 'good guy'); management has come to be portrayed as the outlaw sliding into town in the customary black hat (i.e. the 'bad guy').

It is important to recognize the different emphases and values each brings, but equally they need to be blended together and intertwined to work effectively together. As Allan Lind has observed, 'both are necessary. If you just have management, it is boring. If you just have leadership, it is exciting, but it is scary. If you do both together, then people feel safe but excited at the same time'. Finally, we should resist the trap of ghettoizing leaders and managers, demarcating those who should lead and those who should manage. We agree with Lester Levy when he remarks, 'in each individual you need to have the mind of a manager and the soul of a leader'.

▸▸▸▸ how the book is organized

Given the vast scale of the leadership literature it would be impossible to distil every word that has been written about leadership in a book of even conventional length. In the Appendix we have included some excellent reference sources which can provide such a comprehensive review of leadership research. However, given the space constraints implied by the 'very short' promise in the title of this book, we've decided not to rehearse the history of the theoretical development of leadership studies.

This departs from the strong historic focus of Chris Grey's original book on studying organizations (Grey, 2005). Our reasoning is that any standard organizational behaviour (OB) textbook will do a sound job of providing a historical overview of the development of leadership theories. These accounts invariably begin with what Buchanan and Huczynski (2006) in their own OB text describe as the 'trait spotting' theories of leadership, which attempt to identify personality traits with a view to selecting leaders – much as we did in the section above on what makes an effective leader. They then move on to the 'style counselling' theories which characterize and develop appropriate leadership behaviour patterns, invariably divided into task and relationship orientations. Following this they examine 'context fitting' or contingency theories which emphasize the need to change leadership styles in order to adapt to a particular situation. The situation here invariably incorporates factors such as the state of employee morale, the complexity of the task, and the level of senior management support. Conventional accounts of leadership theories inevitably conclude with a discussion of 'new' leadership theories, which emphasize visionary and inspirational leadership in order to transform organizations (i.e. transformational versus transactional leadership theories). These will primarily be the focus of the next chapter though, technically speaking, they are no longer very new.

What we've chosen to do instead is look at some of the more interesting questions that are currently being asked by those who are studying leadership. While we are not suggesting that one should consider studying only what is currently being studied by other leadership researchers, when one pursues postgraduate studies it is generally wiser to at least begin where other scholars are currently theorizing and proceed from there.

In common with Chris Grey we have taken a very personal view on this subject that is so near and dear to our hearts. We have endeavoured to write this book in a direct, concise and opinionated way using relatively simple language. You will see that we have attempted to keep the academic terminology to a minimum. We are well aware that many students can be initially put off by the dense conceptual language that is used by academics to communicate with each other and conclude that perhaps leadership research or academic research in general is not for them. In this book we want to provide a bridge into this literature and, in the process, show you that there may very well be a place for you. In fact, you may well be able to make a contribution to the literature sooner than you imagine.

We also want to help you develop your critical appreciation of some of the very fine work that is being done in this area but rarely receives any exposure beyond academe. By endeavouring to make this book 'short, interesting and cheap' we realize that we have made a trade-off with the precision, sophistication and depth that you will find in more conventional academic treatises on leadership. Again, for those who wish to consult with more authoritative academic sources we strongly encourage you to begin with the ones we have listed in the Appendix.

In Chapter 2 we will focus on leader-centred perspectives on leadership. The chapter begins with a discussion about the relationship between the identity of a leader and his or her behaviour, and includes a consideration of the influence of gender on leadership. It then contrasts transactional, transformational and charismatic leadership and explores both the 'light' and 'dark' sides of these forms of leadership. These three conceptions of leadership have been the central preoccupation of most leadership researchers in the past two decades. It is this work that most people outside the field identify as being leadership research; indeed the bulk of research papers and postgraduate theses still fall within this particular bailiwick.

Subsequent chapters focus on research that has been done in response to the perceived shortcomings and limitations of this work. In Chapter 3 we survey work done by those who have been curious about that other generally unheralded group of people when it comes to leadership, namely the followers. We specifically look at various theories that have conceptualized followers as moderators or constructors, or substitutes or co-producers of leadership. This work has sought to provide a much needed rebalancing of a lopsided focus on leaders. This is somewhat surprising as most of us are, and always will be, followers and yet Western society tends to take a 'second best' view of followership despite the fact that we all know it – and we all play a vital role in the leadership equation.

In Chapter 4 we bring culture into our analysis. Most of the extant leadership research has been conducted within the United States. It is research that has been done by American researchers predominantly on American subjects, working in American organizations. The growing interest in leadership research throughout the rest of the world has revealed contributions as well as limitations in the applicability and relevance of this research to other national and local contexts. In response, a subfield of leadership research, generally described as cross-cultural leadership, has emerged which has endeavoured to address this issue by seeking explanations for cultural variation in leadership behaviour. However, others have argued that it is not just the specificity of the cultures being explored but the culturally specific way in which they have been explored that has limited our abilities to understand the full range and depth of leadership practices throughout the world.

In Chapter 5, entitled 'Critical Perspectives on Leadership', we look at attempts by various theorists to develop 'leaderful' leadership models which enable followers to take on leadership responsibilities either at the top of the organization, through co- or shared leadership models or throughout the organization through the creation of dispersed leadership models. We take this argument one stage further by considering the possibility of doing away with the idea of leadership altogether and giving it a well-deserved retirement.

In Chapter 6, 'Leadership with a Higher Purpose', we look at a series of related efforts to rehabilitate and invigorate leadership in response to widespread concerns brought into dramatic relief by a number of corporate scandals that erupted in the first part of the century, most infamously with the spectacular and very public collapse of Enron. We may have done a good job at improving leaders' abilities to influence their followers, but what kind of job have we been doing in leading them to do the right thing? Three rapidly growing areas of leadership scholarship are examined which have sought to respond to the shortcomings of mainstream leadership: ethical leadership, authentic leadership, and spiritual leadership. The chapter closes with a consideration of how a more aesthetically informed approach to leadership might improve our understanding and the practice of leadership, particularly when we look at it through the lens of the arts.

Finally in the concluding chapter, Chapter 7, we look at what is being done – in light of all the research that has been presented in the preceding chapters – to develop more and better leaders throughout the world. We look at the still nascent field of leadership development, identifying the conventional means by which leaders are developed, as well as the limitations of these methods. We also consider how you might best prepare and position yourself to become an active contributor in advancing this still young, but rapidly expanding field. To this end, we provide some guidance and advice about what you can do develop your abilities as a student of leadership, most particularly how you might begin to construct your own leadership research – be it a project, a thesis or a dissertation.

For now, content yourself with the knowledge that you are making a good start in this endeavour by reading the rest of this 'very short, fairly interesting and reasonably cheap book about studying leadership'.

2

Leader-centred Perspectives on Leadership

'If we know all too much about our leaders we know far too little about leadership'.

James MacGregor Burns

'[They are] sheep, mere sheep ... easily dispersed if we strike the shepherd'.
Attributed to King Edward the Longshanks
(long-legged), circa 1298

leader identity and leader behaviour

It seems sensible to start a discussion about leadership with a discussion about the leader. In fact, leadership research has been dominated by an interest in leaders. To be specific, research has looked at who the leader is (leader identity), and what the leader does (leader behaviour). In fact, these two issues are still very important in leadership research. We shall first say a few words about leader identity, then move on to leader behaviour.

All textbooks on leadership seem to commence with a treatise on the trait approach. As a courtesy to thirty years of good-quality publishing, we should do so as well. The trait approach seeks to determine the personal qualities and characteristics of leaders. This orientation implies a belief that leaders are born rather than made – in other words, nature is more important than nurture. As we saw in the introductory chapter, Bruce Avolio has been active in researching the nature–nurture debate with regard to the development of leaders. Refreshingly, the conclusion seems to be that it is a 50–50 bet. Yes, heredity and pedigree determine some elements of leadership, but the experiences that we have at home and in life determine our leadership capabilities just as much.

Early research tended to be concerned with the qualities that distinguished leaders from non-leaders or from followers. For many writers concerned with leadership, the findings of such research had implications for their area of interest because of a belief that the traits of leaders would distinguish effective from less effective leaders. In general, the simplicity of the trait theory has reduced its attractiveness for scholars and, since the 1940s, a more persuasive trend has shifted to the examination of leadership behaviour. In summary, the trait approach to leadership has had problems, has been discredited, and is really not valid now.

What does happen in the modern era is a continued assumption that the person in charge is the leader, and therefore is the subject of leadership research and scholarship. We have found that this potential problem of confusing the manager-in-charge with the 'leader' is more prevalent in North America, but is nonetheless an issue all round the world. We have had confusing and at times sometimes frustrating conversations with colleagues, usually in the USA, who claim to be researching 'leadership', and they keep talking about the 'leader'. When pressed further, they are actually talking about the manager of the work unit. It all gets confusing when we are not sure whether we are studying leadership, or a leader, or the manager. It might be splitting hairs, but the basis of the research needs to be clear from the start. The value is that if you say that the person in charge is the leader, then at least you know who you are talking about. What you are probably saying is that the person in charge has the greatest leadership role to play in their management responsibility. That is a perfectly sound premise upon which to base your investigation, and is an important basis for your research.

One problem with this research direction is the implication that you either are a leader or are not. If you don't have the right demographic characteristics or even the right rank in the hierarchy, then you cannot be the leader. Another challenge could be that if you are the manager in charge, you must be the leader, and if you are not the manager then you have no leadership role to play. This dichotomy can be a huge burden to bear for the (unfortunate) person who happens to be the manager in charge of a work unit.

Another problem is that people other than the manager-in-charge do demonstrate leadership from time to time; and from time to time the manager-in-charge is a follower rather than a leader. Therefore, research questions can be confused as a result of this potential dislocation between research subject (manager) and research phenomenon (leadership). It is partly because of this dislocation that we must move now from leader identity to leader behaviour.

The implication of concentrating on leader behaviour rather than leader identity is that the leader can get better at her leadership role by behaving in the most appropriate way. If you strike the right balance between concern for people and concern for production, you will be the most effective leader. Other ways that this balance has been articulated include employee-centred versus production-centred; supportive versus directive; consideration versus initiating structure; relationship-oriented versus task-oriented. These labels pepper the organizational behaviour textbooks and are all talking essentially about the same dichotomy. Some taxonomies of leader behaviours can be quite complex, but the point has been well and truly established that the most effective leaders achieve a balance between the twin challenges of getting the job done and looking after the welfare of the workers.

The behavioural approach to leadership has also gone out of favour in recent years, with the exception that transformational leadership has been criticized as another behavioural theory under a different guise. We will say more about that later.

gender and leadership

In the previous chapter, we referred to the three most commonly asked questions about leadership. If we had included a fourth it would most definitely have been the one that asks: 'What differences are there between male and female leaders?'. The trait approach to leadership seemed to say that men were better leaders than women. The behavioural approach now seems to suggest that women demonstrate better leadership than men do, on average.

Actually, there is no consensus in the literature about gender differences in leadership styles. For example, only weak evidence exists suggesting that women display more transformational leadership than men. Examples include Eagly and Johnson's 1990 meta-analysis and Bass and Avolio's 1994 research. Another meta-analysis is Eagly et al.'s 2003 work on transformational leadership research which revealed a slight but significantly more frequent display of transformational leadership by women over men, across a large number of studies.

Some of our research in New Zealand also found this. When surveying 2,000 managers across the country, we found that irrespective of the gender of the rater, women are seen to display up to 10 per cent more leadership than men, on average. Interestingly, when women fill out the questionnaire, they also are more likely to tick the boxes at the extreme ends of the scale. On the other hand, men are more likely to go for the mid-point ratings. Women are more likely to say that the subject 'never' demonstrates a sense of power or 'always' demonstrates a sense of power. Men are more likely to say that the subject demonstrates a sense of power 'sometimes' or 'fairly often'. Perhaps husbands and boyfriends can empathize with these rather consistent findings. Perhaps wives and girlfriends can empathize with the finding that men are less likely to have a strong view or take a judgemental stand.

Some studies point to gender differences in particular behaviours. For example, Astin and Leland (1992) found that women believe more strongly than men that listening to and empowering followers is important, and women are more likely to use conferences and networks to achieve results. Burke and McKeen suggest that such differences occur because men and women view the world differently, and consequently male leaders seek autonomy and control over their followers while women favour connection and relatedness. It is a complex area and a clear resolution of the issues does not appear to be forthcoming.

Eagly's (1987) social role theory suggests that to avoid criticism and to achieve praise, people behave consistently with society's expectations of their gender. Therefore as leaders, women will strive to be nurturing and caring, while men will be more task-focused, ambitious and competitive. In a large-scale meta-analysis of organizational, laboratory and assessment centre studies, Eagly and Johnson (1990) reported small, but reliable gender differences in leadership style. Female leaders were found to emphasize both interpersonal relations and task accomplishment more than men. Behavioural theory would, therefore, conclude that women are better leaders. However, these differences reduced considerably among organizational leaders vis-à-vis leaders at lower levels. The problem with such small statistical differences is that the significant minority of people who do not conform to stereotype are unfairly labelled with the characteristics of the majority. After all, the 'feminization' of leadership is equally applicable to men as it is to women.

As far back as the early 1990s, many commentators have called for the feminization of leadership as a way to improving long-term organizational effectiveness and well-being. The 'feminization' of leadership does not mean that women are better leaders than men. It means that leaders who conform to the feminized stereotype, that of balance between relationship-orientation and task-orientation, will be the better leaders, irrespective of whether they are women or men.

Eagly and Johnson's findings suggest that leadership processes might vary according to the gender composition of the workplace as much as by the gender dominance of the industry. For example, Chatman and O'Reilly (2004) found that women expressed greater commitment, positive affect and perceptions of cooperation when they worked in all-female groups. Walker et al. (1996) found that in mixed sex groups, men were much more likely to exercise opinion leadership than women. Gardiner and Tiggemann (1999) found that women and men in male-dominated industries did not differ in their interpersonal leadership orientation, however women in female-dominated industries were more interpersonally oriented than men. Furthermore, women exhibiting an interpersonal-oriented leadership style in male-dominated industries reported worse levels of mental health. This finding suggests that both the gender of leader as well as the gender ratio of the industry in general affects leadership styles, although the findings are inconclusive overall.

Clearly, one future direction for research is to assess the impact on leadership of gender domination in the workplace and within the industry generally. On the one hand, the matter of gender and leadership seems to provide a fertile area for research and scholarship (Adler, 1996; Holmes and Marra, 2004; Sinclair, 2005). On the other hand, we suggest that if all these esteemed researchers can come to no consensus about the thorny question of gender and leadership, then perhaps we are asking the wrong question. Ken has a mantra that if you can't find an answer to a question, then you are probably asking the wrong question. This claim relates to the study of leadership as much as to life in general.

What does seem clear is that research in this area appears to be the domain of ageing male and female baby boomers trying to remedy the ills of the past. Experience suggests that Generation X and Y researchers have a different interest in studying gender issues within the phenomenon of leadership, if any interest at all. They would look at powerful women such as Margaret Thatcher, Anita Roddick and Hillary Clinton and agree that issues such as power and communication are more influential than gender for the success of their leadership.

Ken often cites some fascinating work undertaken by Jenny Neale, in the late 1990s. Jenny was part of a multinational study, which investigated the life stories of men and women who had made it to 'the top' as leaders in their industries (Neale, 2001). She looked specifically at Australia and New Zealand. She found that people who made it to the top had in common the privilege of having someone else to look after their domestic situation, such that they could concentrate on their careers. Men invariably had a wife to look after their domestic situation. Unless they were independently wealthy, women did not have a husband to look after their domestic situation. Therefore, those women had foregone a domestic situation by not having children and/or not having a husband. One interpretation of this phenomenon is that leadership success was a function of power rather than gender. To be sure, there has always been a correlation between gender and access to power, but that correlation is becoming weaker all the time.

We have noticed that contemporary research appears to look at gender as a moderator rather than as a dependent or independent variable. As the twenty-first century unfolds, it appears that the characteristics of the individual workplace and the expectations of workforces will have more impact on leadership than does the gender of leaders. The bottom line is that gender differences with regard to leadership, even if significant, are slight. There seems to be little mileage in pursuing this as a specific research direction, unless gender is couched as a social identity rather than as a biological binary relationship.

transformational leadership

One approach to leadership research that has dominated the literature since the 1980s is transformational leadership. It has been hailed, somewhat unfairly, by some people as another behavioural theory of leadership. Transformational leadership is part of what Alan Bryman has called the 'new leadership'. Apart from the fact that new leadership is no longer strictly new, it has generated a great deal of excellent as well as mediocre research and acts as a powerful touchstone for many contemporary leadership researchers. For this reason, the term 'new' still holds some currency.

'New leadership' describes and categorizes a number of approaches to leadership which emerged in the 1980s and exhibited common, or at least similar, themes. Together these different approaches seemed to signal a new way of conceptualizing and researching leadership and they are still going strong. Writers employed a variety of terms to describe the new kinds of leadership which they were concerned with promoting. Among many others, Bass, Avolio, Alimo-Metcalfe, and Tichy and Devanna wrote about 'transformational leadership'. House and Conger wrote persuasively about 'charismatic leadership'. Sashkin, Westley and Mintzberg wrote about 'visionary leadership.' Finally, others such as Bennis, Nanus, Kotter, Kouzes and Posner simply wrote about 'leadership' usually vis-à-vis 'management'. We will say more about charismatic leadership in the next section.

Together these labels revealed a conception of the leader as someone who defines organizational reality through the articulation of a vision, and the generation of strategies to realize that vision. Thus, the new leadership approach is underpinned by a depiction of leaders as what Smircich and Morgan (1982) described as 'managers of meaning'. Another persuasive distillation of the essence of leadership is that of 'sense-making', made famous by Karl Weick in 1995 and articulated further by Annie Pye in 2005. A third distillation of the essence of leadership is that of 'enhancing adaptability' (Parry, 1999). This third essence of leadership is not as famous as the first two, but the point is that the underlying nature of leadership has been explained as more than just an influence process that one imposes upon followers. Of course, arguably the most popular essence of leadership is that of the transformation – a transformation in the attitudes and motivations, and consequently behaviours, of followers – which is generally termed 'transformational leadership'.

The all-important foil for transformational leadership is transactional leadership. Transactional leadership involves an exchange between the leader and follower wherein the leader offers rewards in return for compliance and performance. The transaction is usually represented in formal contracts, employment agreements, performance management systems and service-level agreements. As with behavioural theories of leadership, the most effective leaders are successful at enacting the transformation *and* the transaction. Transformational leadership theory owes a great deal to the ground-breaking work of Bernard Bass, often in partnership with his colleague of many years Bruce Avolio.

Bass's research on transactional and transformational leadership

For Bass, the ideal approach to leadership exhibits both forms of leadership – transformational and transactional. Bass developed quantitative indicators for each component. His specification of these components has varied somewhat as his model has undergone development. The seemingly simple dichotomy of transformation and transaction has been modified through richer and more detailed research to now reflect three higher-order factors that give greater richness to the transformation and transaction. According to Avolio et al. (1999b), the leadership factors are:

Transformational leadership
Inspirational and visionary – developing a vision, engendering pride, respect and trust; creating high expectations, modelling appropriate behaviour.

Intellectual stimulation – continually challenging followers with new ideas and approaches; using symbols to focus efforts.

Developmental exchange (part-transformation and part-transaction)
Individualized consideration – giving personal attention to followers, giving them respect and responsibility, always developing them.
Contingent reward – rewarding followers for conformity with performance targets.
Corrective avoidant (transactional)
Management-by-exception (Active) – looking for mistakes or exceptions to expected behaviour and then taking corrective action.

Passive avoidant – waiting for mistakes to occur before intervening, abdicating leadership responsibility.

Each of these components is measured with the Multifactor Leadership Questionnaire (MLQ). If you are into structural equation modelling, the above factor structure was replicated in a national survey undertaken by Ken at the Centre for the Study of Leadership in New Zealand. Empirically, as well as conceptually and theoretically, this is a powerful way to explain transformational leadership.

The MLQ has a self-rating version, a team version and a conventional leader-rating version. The research, which has been conducted on a host of different levels of leader in a variety of settings, typically shows transformational leadership and developmental exchange to be the components of leader behaviour that are most strongly associated with desirable outcomes such as the performance of subordinates, followers and colleagues. Too much corrective avoidant leadership will result in reduced performance and reduced goal attainment.

Programmes for the selection and training of leaders which draw on this conceptualization and measurement of transactional and transformational leadership have been developed (Bass and Avolio, 1990), as have CDs aimed as spreading the word to managers about transformational leadership (Parry, 2004). Phil Podsakoff also developed a questionnaire to test for six factors of transformational leadership and four factors representing contingent and non-contingent reward, and contingent and non-contingent punishment (Podsakoff et al., 1990). Podsakoff's six transformational leadership factors are: articulates vision, provides appropriate role model, fosters the acceptance of goals, communicates high performance expectations, provides individualized support, and intellectual stimulation. Like Bass's original operationalization of transformational and transactional leadership, these are pitched mainly at the individual level of analysis.

Alimo-Metcalfe and Alban-Metcalfe (2001) also developed a Transformational Leadership Questionnaire (TLQ). This questionnaire measures nine factors, once again at the individual level of analysis and measuring 'close' or 'nearby' leadership, as opposed to 'distant' leadership. Those nine transformational leadership factors are: genuine concern for others; empowers and develops potential; integrity, trustworthy, honest and open; accessibility and approachability; clarifies boundaries, involves others in decisions; encourages critical and strategic thinking; inspirational networker and promoter; decisiveness, determination, self-confidence; and political sensitivity and skills. Once again, they have been adapted for the selection and training of leaders.

Importantly, Bass's and Podsakoff's measures of leadership contain a transactional component as well as a transformational one. Kouzes and Posner's (1998) and Alimo-Metcalfe and Alban-Metcalfe's (2001) measures do not. Waldman et al. (1990) drew attention to the importance of the augmentation effect of transformational leadership over and above the effect of transactional leadership. In other words, as the old mantra says, 'transactional leadership is necessary, but not sufficient'. The transaction seems to be the basis of human interactions. However, it is the transformation, in addition to the transaction, that enables followers to perform beyond expectations. This finding has been supported by Deanne den Hartog and colleagues in 1997, with questionnaire analysis. These theoretical findings, that transactional leadership by itself is necessary but not sufficient for optimal organizational performance, support the conceptual conclusions of Kotter (1990) and others that 'leadership' without 'management' is insufficient for optimal organizational performance.

The idea of transformational leadership has generated an impressive set of findings and has made a great impact on the study of leadership. Given the volume and impact of transformational and 'new' leadership, it is clear that it won't go away in a hurry. Indeed, we believe that it will remain a key component of the study of leadership for many years yet. Some reflections about the new leadership approach can be found in the following overview.

the limitations of transformational and new leadership

With the exception of the research stemming directly or indirectly from Bass's work, the new leadership approach can be accused of concentrating excessively on top leaders. While a switch toward the examination of the leadership *of,* rather than *in,* organizations is in contrast to the small-scale, group-level studies of earlier eras, it could be argued that the change in focus has gone too far and risks having little to say to the majority of leaders. Also, as with earlier phases of research, the new leadership has little to say about informal leadership processes, although the qualitative case studies that have grown in popularity have great potential in this regard. On the other hand, quantitative approaches exhibited by the work of Bass, Podsakoff, Alimo-Metcalfe and Alban-Metcalfe, and Kouzes and Posner, are likely to replicate the tendency to focus on formally designated leaders.

Finally, there has been little situational analysis until recently. Much effort was exerted in the late 1990s toward testing the situational validity of the new leadership, transformational leadership in particular. Attention has been drawn to a wide range of contextual factors that can limit the room for manoeuvre of prospective transformational leaders. These contextual factors might include technology, industry structure, the international trading environment, national public policy, and social and cultural transformation. We have no doubt that many moderating and mediating variables can be tested upon the relationship between transformational leadership and outcome variables.

However, further research along these lines will just be toying with what we already understand, and will probably add little to the body of knowledge. Therefore, there is growing evidence that situational constraints may be much more important in restricting the transformational leader's room for manoeuvre than is generally appreciated. On the other hand, Bass (1997) is insistent that transformational leadership works in almost any situation, except that the way in which it works is, very definitely, situationally contingent. There is a tendency for new leadership writers to emphasize the exploits of successful leaders, and to engage in insufficient examination of the reasons for the loss of transformational attribution. This can generate a distorted impression since there may be important lessons to be learned from failed transformational leaders.

Apart from these concerns, Gary Yukl has typically provided the most cogent critique of transformational leadership theories (Yukl, 1999). One weakness he identifies is the omission of the specification of important behaviours and ambiguity about other transformational behaviours. In part, this criticism has led to the development of Alimo-Metcalfe and Alban-Metcalfe's transformational leadership questionnaire, with a broader range of leadership behaviours and interactions with followers.

Another weakness was insufficient identification of the negative effects of transformational leadership. This shortfall has in part been rectified by Bass and Steidlmeier's (1999) examination of authentic and inauthentic transformational leadership, and also by discussion by Maccoby (2000) and Kets de Vries and Miller (1985) and others on the problems of narcissism with people in senior leadership positions. A third weakness was ambiguity about the underlying influence processes associated with transformational leadership.

We expect that the greater use of qualitative methods to research leadership will remedy these perceived weaknesses over time. A final weakness identified by Yukl (1999) was an overemphasis on dyadic processes of transformational leadership. Once again, the greater use of qualitative methods to research leadership, as a social process found generally within organizations, should move researchers toward a resolution of this problem. Either way, there are still many opportunities for broadening out research into leadership as transformation. We invite you to play your part.

We keep waiting for the transformational leadership 'bubble' to burst and for it to be relegated to the historical scrap-bin as another management fad. However, Ken in particular continues to find that an appreciation of the notion of transformation and transaction is a powerful diagnostic and learning tool for managers and executives in executive development forums. Once people get the point, and it is an easy point to get, the leadership learning really takes off.

There are good reasons to continue studying the new leadership, and transformational leadership in particular. First, it is a well-worked area of research so there is a large body of theory upon which to build. Second, it has been dominated by questionnaire-based research, so there is a good opportunity to broaden the methodological base upon which this research is conducted. Certainly, a continued use of questionnaire research will be expected but, as we have suggested, people have an opportunity to research the contexts within which they live and work in order to gain understanding about the processes that are at play in the leadership that they are experiencing. Questions about 'what is going on?' will probably dominate the research agenda. Having staked a claim for more qualitative research into leadership, we need to add a rider: we see a need for more triangulation of data. In other words, both qualitative and quantitative data, used concurrently and within a broader framework of qualitative analysis, might well provide the greatest insights over time.

charismatic leadership

As we suggested earlier, charismatic leadership is often thought of as a sibling of transformational leadership. It is also thought by other commentators to be a component of transformational leadership. Either way, it is another important aspect of the new leadership that needs to be considered. Much of the research into charismatic leadership has centred on community or political leadership (i.e. the sociological, psychoanalytic and political approaches), rather than leadership in organizations. The transitory nature of charismatic leadership makes it difficult to isolate and therefore to research. For example, Tony Blair was hugely charismatic in the early years of his prime ministership. By the end of it, his charismatic aura had lost much of its glow. For many 'charismatic' leaders, the gain and loss of charisma happens much faster than the ten years it has taken for Blair to lose his. Even so, striving to understand the process of gaining and losing charisma continues to be a fruitful and underutilized research avenue to explore.

The main approaches that normally attract scholars are the behavioural approach, lionized by Bob House (1977), Bernie Bass (1998) and Jay Conger (1987), the attribution approach, articulated by Jay Conger (as well), Jane Howell, and the great conceptual thinker Boas Shamir (Shamir and Howell, 1999), and the follower self-concept approach (Shamir et al., 1993). Along the same lines, Zaleznik's (1977) and Hummel's (1975) psychoanalytic approach to charisma emphasizes the impact that leaders have on followers. These two follower-centred approaches to understanding leadership will be explored further in Chapter 3.

The key variable is the motivation and response of followers that charismatic leaders can tap into. This approach to leadership is best suited to political leadership; case studies such as Hitler, Gandhi, Mandela and various US presidential candidates are often analysed. Whereas most work on charismatic leadership has focused on the leader behaviours and follower effects as independent and dependent variables, Boas Shamir (1992) has added to the debate by positing an explanation for the intervening variable which links leadership and effect. He suggests that charismatic leadership has its effect by heightening the self-concept of followers. In particular, charismatic leadership generates heightened self-esteem and self-worth, increased self-efficacy and collective efficacy, personal identification with the leader, identification with a prestigious and distinctive social group, and internalization of the values of the leader. Clearly, charisma is a complex psycho-social phenomenon.

Charismatic leadership really is a function of the whole situation. It is leader identity, leader behaviour, follower identity, sociocultural context and organizational setting all working together concurrently. Therefore, one should be researching that whole situation in its entirety to understand what is going on. The topic is perennially sexy. People can readily relate to political, sporting or corporate leadership that has a charismatic effect on followers. As such, charismatic leadership is always relevant to the lives of people in any society. Whether scholars utilize historiography, case study method, phenomenography, biographical analysis, visual ethnography or political psychology the topics are always relevant and entertaining. One just cannot get the feel for charismatic leadership by using the quantitative questionnaire methodology that has otherwise dominated the new leadership. On the other hand, when you discuss charismatic leadership, you cannot avoid the matter of personality and its role in the process.

leadership and personality

This is an issue that has always been best researched psychometrically with questionnaire instruments. Leadership has been linked to certain personality factors in leaders (Judge et al., 2002). Those personality factors are conscientiousness, agreeableness, extraversion and emotional stability. The works of Cable and Judge (2003) and Smith and Canger (2004) are probably good places to start.

It is important to recognize that the links between the demonstration of leadership and personality factors have always been modest, even though they are statistically significant. Certain personalities lend themselves more to demonstrating leadership than others. For example, a person who is organized, reliable and ambitious (high in conscientiousness) is more likely to be seen as a leader than someone who is unreliable and careless (low in conscientiousness). This finding makes sense, but ironically the finding is not strong and it is not universal. In other words, contrary to what we might think intuitively, some less reliable and careless people can and do have leadership attributed to them.

The point is that, irrespective of your personality, you can engage in the behaviours of effective leadership. We would hate to have to say to someone, 'sorry, but because of your personality, you cannot be a leader', or worse, 'sorry, but because of your personality, you cannot be in a leadership position' – or even worse, 'sorry, but you cannot even be better at leadership because you have the wrong personality!'. However, that being said, we believe it is important to be aware of links between personality and leadership. It is important to know how and why certain leader–follower relationships work. Perhaps a future direction for research should be an examination of the relationship between the personality of followers (or workers) and leadership by the manager. Either way, it is important to understand where people are 'coming from', both figuratively and literally. By the same token let's not lose sight of the idea that, in spite of our personality profile, we can *all* learn to become better leaders.

Craig and Gustafson (1998) developed an instrument to assess the perceived integrity of leaders. Not surprisingly, it is called the Perceived Leader Integrity Scale, or PLIS. Ken utilized a modified version of that scale to test the relationship between transformational leadership and perceived integrity in one of his national surveys in New Zealand (Parry and Proctor-Thomson, 2002). As expected, he found a generally positive relationship between perceptions of integrity and attributions of leadership. However, an intriguing side issue he found was that six per cent of leaders in New Zealand organizations were found to be above average in the display of leadership yet below average in perceived integrity. In other words, some people in leadership positions give all the inspirational speeches and get to know the needs of individuals and display a sense of power; yet followers still believe that those leaders lack integrity.

These figures resonate with Gustafson and Ritzer's (1995) and Babiak's (1996) finding that approximately one in twenty managers are aberrant self-promoters, a mild form of organizational psychopath. The implication is that some people are enacting all the right transformational behaviours, yet what is in their heart is not as honourable as they would like their followers to believe. These and related findings have heralded an exciting new direction for research which examines the dark side of personality, rather than the conventional components of the rational personality. The dark side includes among other facets of personality: narcissism, passive-aggressive personality, obsessive-compulsive personality, anti-social behaviour, and paranoid, schizotypal and histrionic personalities. We believe that there are plenty of opportunities for further research. If you have a strong psychological leaning this might be an area that you consider studying further. Not only is this a hugely important area of research for the mental and emotional health of our society, it also seems to be a 'hot button' topic that is guaranteed to attract media attention.

the narcissistic leader

The examination of the narcissistic leader is more than just an extension of the link between personality and leadership. The narcissistic leader has become a separate sub-field of leadership research in its own right. The narcissistic leader has been the subject of much popular press writing. Some well-read examples are books which directly and indirectly address this issue. Narcissistic leaders hold great fascination for the average taxpaying and voting voyeur, especially those naughty narcissistic CEOs. There is more than a whiff of desire and arousal in the power that goes with the lofty levels at which these people operate. The stakes are high.

In one particularly well-cited issue of the *Harvard Business Review*, Michael Maccoby (2000) discussed the 'incredible pros' and the 'inevitable cons' of narcissistic leaders. There are any number of psychology textbooks that explain the narcissistic personality but, for our purposes here, the narcissistic leader is usually represented by the larger-than-life personalities whom we see running organizations and figuring prominently in our society – best personified by the likes of Richard Branson, Donald Trump and Jack Welch.

One strength of the narcissistic leader is their ability to energize followers with a grand and compelling vision. Another strength is to generate large numbers of followers who can enact the vision. In fact, the narcissistic leader is very dependent upon the followers. There are also weaknesses of the narcissistic leader. They are sensitive to criticism.

They are poor listeners. They lack empathy and have a distaste for mentoring although they have an intense desire to compete.

The focus of research into the narcissistic leader could equally be the leader or the followers. A good example of the latter is the study by Elmes and Barry (1999) of narcissistic behaviour exhibited by mountaineering groups on the rock face which ultimately led to the tragic climbing deaths described in the bestseller, *Into Thin Air* (Krakauer, 1997). By the nature of its subject, this research usually takes the form of a case study. The books and popular press on narcissistic leaders are effectively case studies, albeit lacking in empirical rigour. There is room for improvement in the quality of the research that goes into such case studies. Equally, by virtue of the impact of personality on leadership, there is also still great scope for more traditional questionnaire research into the narcissistic leader. In terms of some of the research that has been undertaken, Post (1986), Kets de Vries and Miller (1985), and Maccoby (2000) have discussed the impact of personality aberrations such as narcissism upon the performance of people in senior leadership roles.

the rise of the anti-narcissistic leader

Perhaps the most influential leadership idea to emerge in the popular realm in the first part of the twenty-first century has been the notion of 'level 5' leadership which was coined by Jim Collins in his best-selling business book, *Good to Great* (Collins, 2001a). Continuing the theme of sustainable corporate success that was so profitably mined in his earlier bestseller, *Built to Last* (Collins and Porras, 1995), Jim Collins and his research team set out to discover what underlay the continued superior performance of a handful of American corporations over several decades rather than the short term.

Despite their best efforts not to pin success on the quality of the leadership at the top of the organization, that is in fact what they found. In particular they discovered a CEO at each company who had well and truly paid his dues (they were all males) in the company and the industry steadily, had patiently worked his way to the top of the organization, and was sticking around through thick and thin. By no means overnight sensations, these CEOs represented the antithesis of the charismatic and narcissistic turnaround kings who were held up as the archetypal CEOs during the financial booms of the 1980s and 1990s. Collins suggest that the latter 'magic leaders' exemplified what he terms 'level 4 leadership' – highly effective in the short-term but, due to character flaws, doomed to fail in the longer term. They fall short of 'level 5 leaders' who, by contrast:

are a study in duality: they are modest and willful, shy and fearless. They act with quiet, calm determination and they rely principally on inspired standards, not inspiring charisma, to motivate. They channel their ambition into the company, not the self. They also 'look in the mirror, not the window, to apportion responsibility for poor results, never blaming other people, external factors or bad luck. Similarly, they look out of the window to apportion credit for the company's success to employees, external factors or good luck.

The level 5 leader is personified by Wade Thompson, the co-founder with Peter Orthwein of Thor Industries, the world's largest recreational vehicle company. Since purchasing the iconic but financially ailing Airstream company in 1980, Wade and Peter have slowly but surely built a highly successful company that has become one of America's fifteen most admired companies. They have done this by consistently adhering to a few basic principles rooted in integrity, responsibility and accountability, many of which they share with the legendarily low-key yet spectacularly successful investment guru, Warren Buffet. They have achieved all of this in a studiously understated manner, miles away from the media spotlight. Brad was fortunate to have the opportunity to make a documentary called *The Open Road* which describes the historic growth of this multibillion dollar company as a means to teach the next generation of strategic leaders.

This discernible weather change away from celebrating the 'loud and proud' charismatic leader archetype to a more humble, ethical anti-charismatic leader has also found its way into popular accounts of leadership at other levels within the organization and the community at large. Most notably, Joseph Badaracco (2002) in his book *Leading Quietly* compellingly observes:

> They're not making high stakes decisions. They're often not at the top of organizations. They often don't have the spotlight and publicity on them. They think of themselves modestly; they often don't even think of themselves as leaders. But they are acting *quietly*, effectively, with political astuteness, to basically make things better, sometimes much better than they would otherwise.

Brad and his colleague, Eric Guthey, from the Copenhagen Business School have investigated what they describe as the 'hero manager backlash' that gathered momentum at the beginning of 2002 in the advent of the widely vilified corporate scandals and the burst of the dot.com bubble (Guthey and Jackson, 2005). They trace the media backlash through an analysis of the changing portrayals of CEOs featured on the covers and within the pages of high-profile business periodicals such as *Business Week*, *Fortune* and *Forbes*. They note the tendency of the media to not only seek to demonize heroic leaders, pillorying them in quite shocking visual fashion (after celebrating them only a year prior), but also to find new heroes to replace them. In this regard, they note that the media have replaced the 'Men in Black' level 4 leaders with the 'Men in Beige' level 5 leaders. At what point and in what form these leaders will be subsequently knocked down and replaced by the 'level 6' leaders (whomsoever they may be), is anyone's guess.

As we shall see in Chapter 6, leadership scholars have not been impervious to this tectonic shift in popular attitudes towards business leadership. In Chapter 6 we describe the three-pronged quest for leaders who have a higher purpose (i.e. above the grubby preoccupation with hard cash and absolute power) by exploring authentic, ethical and spiritual leadership. Much of this work has sought to invigorate the theory and practice of transformational yet drive charismatic leadership to the sidelines. Typical of this search is the observation made by Gardner and his colleagues about 'the authentic leader':

We are struck by the uplifting effects of lower profile but genuine leaders who lead by example in fostering healthy ethical climates characterised by transparency, trust, integrity, and high moral standards. We call such leaders authentic leaders who are not only true to themselves, but lead others by helping them to likewise achieve authenticity (Gardner et al. 2005: 344).

Essentially, what we are witnessing here is the continued desire by leadership scholars to solve what are perceived to be problems created by poor leadership by selecting and developing the 'right' type of leader. New leadership theory emphasized the dramatic performance improvements that could be realized by visionary leaders who were able to inspire their followers through their charismatic rather than their formal authority. While results have often been dramatic they have sometimes been achieved with unacceptable ethical, moral and psychological costs. This has caused leadership scholars to shift their focus away from the 'means to the ends' of leadership, specifically to inspect the moral and ethical bases of leadership goals. Their quest for genuinely authentic, ethically sound and spiritually enlightened leaders maintains the leader-centric perspective which endeavours to solve leadership problems by focusing on the leader. The followers, therefore, continue to play a marginal and incidental role. In Chapter 3 we will look at a number of bold but isolated efforts to redress this situation by finally bringing the follower into the analysis.

conclusion

This chapter began with a discussion regarding the relationship between the identity of a leader and his or her behaviour. Related to this we considered the influence of gender on leadership and concluded that, while biologically-oriented research had revealed surprisingly little difference, those who had looked at gender from a social identity perspective had provided comparatively more fertile terrain for leadership researchers. We reviewed the substantial contribution that new leadership theory (encompassing transformational, transactional and charismatic leadership) had made to our understanding of what constitutes effective leadership and how to promote it. We also noted a number of criticisms that have been levelled at this impressive and still highly influential body of work.

In exploring the relationship between personality and leadership, we noted that most research had focused on the positive and rational aspects of personality that were seen to be conducive to fostering good leadership. We also noted and welcomed a growing interest in understanding the 'dark' as well as the 'light' side of leadership personality, pointing specifically to the role of narcissism in promoting good and bad leadership. We closed the chapter by discussing the shift that had taken place in the popular archetypes of sound strategic leadership from the larger-than-life visionary charismatic business leaders of the 1980s and 1990s to the more humble, ethical and understated business leaders of the 2000s, in the aftermath of the corporate scandals and the bursting of the dot.com bubble.

3

Follower-centred Perspectives on Leadership

'New insights into the processes of leadership can be gained by focusing attention squarely on processes connected to followers and their contexts, independently of what leaders are actually doing'

Meindl et al., 2004: 1347

<hr>

introducing the follower

In Chapter 1, we introduced Joseph Rost's definition of leadership as an influence relationship among leaders and followers who intend real changes that reflect their mutual purposes. In Chapter 2 we focused our attention on the leader's role in this relationship. In this chapter we turn to the role of the follower.

At the beginning of the presentation on leadership that Brad gives to undergraduate students he conducts a quick poll. He asks how many of them aspire to be a 'good leader'. Invariably, between 10 and 15 of the class of 200 put up their hands. When he asks how many of them aspire to be good followers, either none or one lone maverick student will put up a hand. This does not change even when Brad puts up his hand – such is the level of influence that he exerts on the class.

Setting aside the concern that the vast majority of undergraduates aspire to be neither a good leader nor a good follower – or at least are not willing to publicly declare their intentions, good or bad – the almost non-existent desire to be a good follower is striking and potentially unsettling. We all know instinctively that we will spend most of our life as a follower and only a small proportion of it as a leader, but it is not something that we are generally proud to admit, let alone celebrate. Even the most powerful world leaders, whether it's the President of the United States, the Pope or even Bono, will spend most of their lives as followers too. In fact, the public is quite amused when it catches prominent leaders acting as followers, whether it's being cajoled by an adviser or a protester or being gently reprimanded by their spouse or children. We all have to follow: as Bob Dylan wryly observes, 'You Gotta Serve Somebody'.

Being reticent or reluctant to follow is not something that is peculiar to undergraduate students but, as will see in Chapter 4 on culture and leadership, is a strong feature of individualistically oriented Western societies, especially those that are characterized by low power distance values. Part of the problem is the word 'follower' itself. Being a follower implies that you are second best, you are not good enough to lead. It implies a measure of servitude, having to become sheep-like or worse – a zombie who is devoid of independent thought, lacking opinion and free will. For some, the notion of following has strong religious overtones suggesting blind devotion which further serves to undermine the currency of the term.

The uneasiness or lack of interest in either talking about or understanding followership, is reflected in how much less the term crops up on the Internet. Karl Weick notes from a Google search that he found 57 items relating to the word 'leader' for everyone regarding a 'follower' (Weick, 2007). This imbalance is reflected in the number of books that are published on the subject. While just over 5,000 non-fiction books could be ordered through Amazon.com with the word 'leadership' in their title, only six books could be ordered with the word 'followership' in their title. The top three best selling of these were *Followership: A Practical Guide to Aligning Leaders and Followers*, *Leadership and Followership: The Cybernetics of University Governance* and *Political Followership in Nigeria*. Before you go online to order these – you should note that the latter two are currently unavailable. Of course, Ken and Brad have done nothing to correct this imbalance. But let's face it, if we were to have entitled this book *A Very Short, Fairly Interesting and Reasonably Cheap Book About Studying Followership* how many of you would have gone ahead and either bought or borrowed this book?

One response to the problem has been to look for alternative terms. Various replacements have been proposed from 'team member' to 'collaborator', 'colleague', 'partner', or even 'peer' – but none of them have caught on in either popular or academic discourse. The word 'follower' persists, albeit with grudging and somewhat embarrassed acceptance, in our leadership lexicon. We will, however, be using the term in this chapter with unbridled enthusiasm as we strive to show that it is not the act of following that is necessarily problematic, indeed it is vital to leadership, but as with leading there are more and less effective ways in which to follow.

The undue primacy that is placed on leaders over followers has been reinforced by leadership scholars. A major exception to this has been Jim Meindl, the Director of the Center for Leadership Studies at the State University of New York, at Buffalo NY Binghamton, who sadly passed away at the peak of his career in 2004. Jim's major contribution to leadership studies was to lead a 'follower-centric' approach to leadership studies offered by way of a much-needed counterweight to an almost exclusive preoccupation with leader-centric approaches. Consolidating earlier arguments made by Pfeffer (1977), Pfeffer and Salancik (1978) and Calder (1977) he observed that, while most leadership scholars would have little difficulty in recognizing that leadership is fundamentally predicated on the relationship between leaders and followers, the follower almost invariably took a minor supporting role in the analysis of leadership.

Reading Jim's work, one is struck by his deep-seated discomfort in the tendency for his peers and his fellow citizens to place such great stock in the role of leaders, especially those at the apex of the organization. This misplaced faith was held despite the overwhelming weight of evidence showing that external forces and a myriad of alternative internal factors are considerably more influential in determining organizational performance. He concluded with more than a hint of resignation that, 'the concept of leadership is a permanently entrenched part of the socially constructed reality that we bring to bear in our analysis of organisations. And there is every sign that the obsessions and celebrations of it will persist' (Meindl, Ehrlich and Dukerich, 1985: 78). The twenty or so years since he made this observation would have only served further to reinforce his conviction.

A recently published book, *Follower-Centered Perspectives on Leadership,* collects together in a tribute to the memory of James Meindl a number of researchers who are actively working on the development of new follower-centric approaches to leadership. In the book's introduction, Boas Shamir provides a helpful overview of this work and identifies five roles that followers have traditionally played in leadership theories: 'followers as recipients of leader influence'; 'followers as moderators of leader impact'; 'followers as substitutes for leadership', 'followers as constructors of leadership' and 'followers as leaders' (2007). We have used these categories to organize our discussion. We will close the chapter by considering a sixth role that Boas and his colleagues have advocated for followers: 'followers as co-producers of leadership'. This perspective has been developed as a critical alternative to the five ways in which followers have been traditionally conceptualized. This is a conceptualization which is very much in tune with our own thinking and is ripe for further study and investigation.

▒▒▒▒▒ followers as recipients of leadership

The passive conception of the follower's role in leadership has been the traditionally dominant view. As such it has done little to challenge the popular stereotypes about followers and followership. As we saw in Chapter 1, traditional leadership theories posit the leader's traits and behaviour as the independent variables and the followers' perceptions, attitudes and behaviours to be explained as the dependent variables in the leadership equation.

Even with the more recent theories of transformational, transactional and charismatic leadership discussed in Chapter 2, the onus is still firmly placed on the leader to create one or a blend of these forms of leadership for the followers to respond to. If the leader follows the correct procedures, he or she will succeed in creating transactional or charismatic or transformational leadership, irrespective of the followers. The way these theories perceive the leadership process, it does not really matter who you are trying to lead. Followers do not play an active role in the leadership process. It is an essentially linear, one-way relationship between leaders and followers. The follower is, in effect, a blank slate upon which the leader writes the script.

▒▒▒▒▒ followers as moderators of leadership

As we saw in the first chapter, contingency theories of leadership acknowledge that the leader's influence on followers' attitudes and performance depends on the individual follower's characteristics. This view of followers still thinks of them as primarily passive recipients of influence, but acknowledges that the leader's influence may have to be moderated by the characteristics of the follower.

Brad recalls from the first leadership training course he took, which was on 'situational leadership' (Hersey and Blanchard, 1977), that he had to learn to change his leadership style depending on the level of 'maturity' of the follower. This was determined by the ability and the motivation of the follower. With an immature follower, he should take on a 'telling style' of leadership in which he would tell the employees what needed to be done but not be too interested in them as people. 'Relationship behaviour' would come later. As the follower became more capable and motivated, Brad could then move to a 'selling style' in which he would keep up the task pressure but could also begin to cultivate a good relationship with the employee.

Moving around the compass, he could then progress to a 'participatory style' in which he could cease to give direction and allow the followers to direct themselves and devote his attention to relationship-building activities. In the final stage, presumably some form of leadership nirvana, Brad could take on a 'delegating leadership style' (more derogatively referred to as 'laissez-faire' leadership), by which he could leave the employees to their own devices and let them lead themselves. This all sounded so enticing in theory, but in practice the followers rarely stuck to the same script. They had obviously been on a different course! They kept throwing up all kinds of complications such as having different opinions, not sharing the same motives and plunging various spanners into the works.

Contingency theorists have pointed to a number of other aspects of followers that leaders need to take into account when leading. These include: the follower's initial attitude toward the leader and their acceptance of the leader (Fiedler, 1967); the follower's needs for either technical or emotional support (House, 1971); and the follower's knowledge and the congruence of their values with their leaders' (Vroom and Yetton, 1973). While each of the theories tries to point to another aspect of the follower that the leader must take into account when determining how to behave, the overriding expectation is for the leader to be the active partner in the leadership process.

followers as substitutes for leadership

From time to time the careers section in the newspaper runs articles publicizing the latest HR consultancy survey, highlighting the finding that the number one reason why most people leave their jobs is because of a bad boss. Money, conditions, benefits and prospects pale into insignificance compared to an abusive or inconsiderate boss it would seem. Leaving is, of course, one way to deal with a bad boss. Another way is to find ways to avoid him or her and minimize the damage.

The 'substitutes for leadership' theory originated by Steven Kerr and John Jermier provides some encouragement in this regard (Kerr and Jermier, 1978). It argues that, under certain conditions, the influence of a leader over a follower may actually be neutralized or even substituted. If it is neutralized, it means that it is impossible for either the task-oriented or the relationship-oriented activities of a leader to make a difference to a follower's attitudes or behaviour. If leadership is substituted, it means that the leader's activities are not only impossible, but they are also largely unnecessary.

Returning to the problem of avoiding a bad boss, those followers who have high levels of ability, experience, training and knowledge – as well as a high need for independence and a strongly 'professional' orientation – tend to have a low need for both the relationship-building and task-oriented activities of the leader. Moreover, when the task at hand is relatively straightforward and routine you have little need for a boss. Alternatively, if you can get into a job that is intrinsically satisfying (such as being a university lecturer perhaps?), or you can see directly what you have achieved such as when you are a paramedic, you do not need a boss to explain to you how important your work is or how you are doing. Finally, you might consider joining an organization which is highly bureaucratic in that the work and the rewards are highly formalized and little is left to the boss's discretion. Best of all, try taking a job in which there is considerable spatial distance between you and your boss, but beware of the remarkable reach of the Blackberry.

Perhaps not surprisingly, the substitutes for leadership theory has strong intuitive appeal for those who do not subscribe to the importance of leadership in organizational processes. It serves quite effectively to take the wind out of the sails of leadership scholars who trumpet the central importance of leadership in organizational success and failure. It has, however, failed to lead to much in the way of subsequent research, serving primarily as an act of protest. A series of exchanges published in *Leadership Quarterly* may, however, succeed in generating further theoretical and methodological refinements to the substitutes for leadership, particularly as it applies to strategic leadership at senior levels within organizations (Dionne, Yammarino, Howell and Villa, 2005).

Boas Shamir characterizes the way in which the substitutes for leadership theory perceives of the follower's role as an extreme version of seeing followers as moderators of leadership. In common with this perspective, the specific activities of followers in substituting for leadership are not actively theorized. The theory has been developed primarily to de-emphasize the significance of the leader but it does not do a lot to explicate the role of followers in creating leadership. As we shall see in the following section, the next group of theories have made this task their central concern.

followers as constructors of leadership

In this section we will talk about research that has examined the way in which followers make or construct leadership. These researchers are preoccupied with the thoughts of followers, most especially how they construct and represent leaders in their thought systems. They make the fundamental point that leadership is essentially in the eye of the follower. Unless followers recognize it as leadership, it isn't leadership. We will distinguish between three groups of theories that have identified a different aspect of this construction process: the romance of leadership theory, the psychodynamic theory of leadership, and the social identity theory of leadership.

the romance of leadership

At the beginning of this chapter we noted that the follower-centric view of leadership emanated from a concern that most leadership scholars had become overly preoccupied with the role of the leader in creating leadership, while virtually ignoring the role of the follower. Essentially, leadership scholars were mirroring and indeed perpetuating, the hype and unrealistic expectations that are routinely placed on leaders in all spheres of human endeavour, but most especially in the world of business and politics. Rather than turn their back on leadership studies, Jim Meindl and his colleagues decided to make this tendency to overestimate the significance of leadership their central concern.

At the heart of their analysis lies the notion of the 'romance of leadership', which they suggest 'denotes a strong belief – a faith – in the importance of leadership factors to the functioning and dysfunctioning of organised systems' (Meindl and Ehrlich, 1987: 91). A series of empirical studies conducted in laboratory settings – through the development of a survey instrument, the Romance of Leadership Scale (RLS) – and the analyses of media reports revealed a consistent pattern of follower behaviour (Meindl and Ehrlich, 1988). In the absence of direct, unambiguous information about an organization, respondents would tend to ascribe control and responsibility to leaders with events and outcomes to which they could be plausibly linked (Meindl et al. 1985). In effect, leadership acted as a simplified, biased and attractive way to make sense of organizational performance. Moreover, this romantic tendency seemed to have the greatest sway in extreme cases – when things were going either extremely well or extremely badly observers tended to lay the credit or blame at the foot of the leader.

Meindl did not advance the follower-centric approach in an effort either to compete or to replace the dominant leader-centric approach. As Meindl noted: 'Rather than being anti-leadership, the romance of leadership, and the perspective it provides, is more accurately portrayed as an alternative to theories and perspectives that place great weight on "leaders" and on the substantive significance to their actions and activities' (1995: 330). Looked at through the romance of leadership lens you could see that perhaps superior performance was, in fact, the cause and not the consequence of charismatic leadership (Awamleh and Gardner, 1999: 346). Put succinctly, leaders keep on winning largely because their followers perceive them to be winners. They, therefore, do everything they can to ensure this continues to be the case; for example,

Manchester United players would do everything they could to keep Sir Alex Ferguson in his winning ways.

Meindl described the romance of leadership as a social construction. Followers construct their opinion about the leader by interacting with other followers. Central to this process is something he called social contagion, which he described as 'a phenomenon of the spontaneous spread of affective and/or behavioural reactions among the members of a group or social collective' (Meindl, 1993: 101). As its name suggests, we can think of a leader's reputation (good or bad) as being something akin to influenza that can be passed on from follower to follower until everyone becomes infected. Social contagion highlights the interpersonal processes and group dynamics that underpin the widespread dissemination of charismatic effects among followers and subordinates.

The media are important contributors to these social construction and social contagion processes. Media accounts influence and shape the attributions that followers might give to a particular leader. They can also shape our general beliefs about what constitutes effective and ineffective, ethical and unethical leadership. These processes are illustrated to good effect in an empirical study, based on media accounts, conducted by Chen and Meindl (1991) of the career of People Express founder and chief executive Donald Burr. Burr's airline enjoyed a brief but highly celebrated heyday before encountering insurmountable financial problems and folding into Texas Air just five short years after it made its inaugural flight in 1981 in a blaze of publicity. The study shows how the press collectively constructed Donald Burr as an idealized representation of the American entrepreneurial spirit, infused with vision and inspiration in the manner of a pioneering evangelical preacher. They stuck with this image of the leader throughout the life of the company but made a marked switch – in the face of sustained poor company performance – from celebrating the positive connotations associated with this image to revealing its negative connotations.

Chen and Meindl conclude that, contrary to popular wisdom, leaders do not control their own destiny despite the best efforts of public relations professionals. Brad knows this only too well from his time as a 'spin doctor'. The identity and influence of leaders depends to a large extent on the manner in which their followers perceive them. Both leaders and followers are subject to a range of forces beyond their direct control; prominent among them are the dynamics of the news industries that disseminate information about leaders to their followers and the wider society. The business media, in turn, are subject to a variety of internal and external pressures. They have to sell newspapers and advertising space and, therefore, have to influence their readers and various other stakeholders. Consequently, they play to our hunger for personalized news in the belief that individual leaders control the fate of organizations rather than relational or structural forces. In constructing leader images, they match the leader's characteristics with the performance of the firm. Consequently, the CEO of a successful firm will tend to be depicted with positive personal qualities, and vice versa.

The 'celebrity CEO' phenomenon takes full advantage of our tendencies to romanticize leadership. In an increasingly complicated and impersonal world, the public face of a charismatic and appealing CEO can prove to be a highly effective means for a company to build a symbolic link or brand with its various stakeholders, such as its shareholders, its customers or its suppliers. A 'real' person provides the human touch that cannot be provided by a mere logo. It is almost impossible to not think about Richard Branson without thinking about the Virgin brand and vice versa. Having a celebrity CEO at the helm can act as a double-edged sword, however. It is difficult to maintain confidence in an organization once the influential founder moves on, as The Body Shop found when Anita Roddick gave up control of the company. It's even more of a challenge when your founder goes to jail, as was demonstrated in spectacular fashion with the imprisonment of Martha Stewart. Redemption can be a powerful motivator as witnessed by the impressive turnaround in Martha Stewart Living Omnimedia, Inc. since her release.

The romance of leadership theory is particularly strong in describing a tendency for followers to exaggerate the importance and influence of the leader in determining a group or organization's performance. If things are going well, it's the leader's doing; if things are going badly, that is also the leader's doing. The theory also provides some useful insights into how this takes place, with its exposition of social construction and social contagion processes. Where the theory is not as strong is in explaining why this happens. The following two theories – psychoanalytic theory and social identity theory – provide pointers as to why followers might choose to construct leadership in the way they have been observed to do.

pyschoanalytic theories

When we addressed the question regarding leaders being born or made in the opening chapter we pointed to the importance of our early years in shaping and defining our individual philosophies of leadership. Psychoanalytic theories of leadership take this observation several steps further.

Rooted in Sigmund Freud's psychoanalysis and Carl Jung's psychopathology, the psychodynamic approach highlights the centrality of our family of origin if we wish to understand our behaviour, whether as a leader or as a follower (Stech, 2004). A leader's style is heavily influenced by the models of leadership exhibited by parents, teachers, coaches and other adults during the maturation process from child, through adolescent, to adulthood. Most potent of these is the style of parenting, particularly very early in the impressionable years (Keller, 2003). An adult might choose to copy that parent's style or may choose a diametrically opposite style. We often see someone who was raised in an authoritarian way consciously reject this approach in favour of a more laissez-faire approach. One is, however, struck when confronted with the actual challenge of raising a child, how those familiar patterns emerge – despite our best intentions.

The way in which we are raised also influences the way in which we choose to follow. If adults find themselves in a relationship with either an authoritarian leader or a leader with a more participative style, the reaction of the adult may be influenced by the way their authority figures, parents in particular, behaved and dealt with authority figures in the past.

Psychodynamically, we may react to a leader in either a dependent, a counter-dependent or an independent manner (Stech, 2004). We might become totally dependent on the leader for our livelihood and our emotional support. When we react in a counter-dependent way we react rebelliously, rejecting the directives of the leader. As an independent follower we look at the leader's directive objectively, assessing whether or not it is reasonable and ethical, before choosing to act. It is this type of followership behaviour that responsible leaders actively try to encourage in their followers. Dealing with chronically dependent and counter-dependent followers presents two different sets of challenges that can prove to be gruelling and very painful to address for both parties.

In explaining why followers construct leaders in a dependent way, psychoanalytic theories of leadership point to two psychodynamic processes: projection and transference (Shamir, 2007). Projection is the process by which we attribute to another person our ideals, wishes, desires and fantasies. We see this tendency being demonstrated by diehard fans of pop stars, actors and models. Transference, on the other hand, is the process of responding to another person as if that person was one's mother, father or another significant person from early childhood.

Pyschoanalytic theories suggest that these processes are particularly salient during periods of crisis or threat; when people are confused, unsafe or helpless, followers can regress to early childhood patterns and behaviour. They become attached to leaders and idealize and obey them, not because of the leader's special characteristics but because the leader symbolizes a father, a mother or some omnipotent figure. Citing Freud's writings on leadership (Freud, 1921), George Goethals suggests that strong male leaders such as George Washington have the ability to reawaken unconscious archaic images of the powerful male ('The Big

Man') who ruled despotically over primitive human societies. Taking up Darwin's notion of the 'primal horde', Freud argued that the father or chief was a strong and independent figure who imposed his will on all other members of the group. Followers had the illusion that their leader loved each of them equally.

Leaders can also provide a means by which the follower can reduce their level of anxiety and provide them with a measure of psychological safety. In order to meet these pyschological needs followers, through the processes of transference or projection, will sometimes knowingly tolerate – sometimes prefer and even create – 'toxic leaders'. Jean Lipman-Blumen notes that 'toxic leaders manipulate their followers' ordinary human needs and exploit their existential circumstances. They do this by creating illusions designed to allay the fears and address the human condition to which we all are heir' (2007: 3). By the same token, Lynn Offerman (2004) alerts us to the various ways in which 'toxic followers' might similarly lead their leaders astray.

Cult leaders such as Charles Manson, Jim Jones and David Koresh are held up as infamous prime exemplars of this form of deleterious leadership which Micha Popper likens to a process of mass hypnosis in which followers lose their self and the ability to reason autonomously (Popper, 2001). We can also see elements of this process in more conventional leader–follower relationships. Brad's doctoral research, for example, examined why so many managers chose to follow such mamagement gurus as Stephen Covey, Michael Hammer and Peter Senge.

The psychodynamic approach to leadership is by no means a mainstream approach within the study of leadership. Leadership scholars share the same general discomfort and reticence about working with the unconscious mind that psychologists tend to have. Critics point to the approach's origins in the clinical observation and treatment of people with serious difficulties, not those whom we tend to find in typical workplaces. The theory is also based on the subjective findings of clinical psychologists collected from individual case studies; it is not based on conventional scientific principles. In defence, Manfred Kets de Vries observes with typical irony, 'it's something of a paradox that, while at a conscious level we might deny the presence of unconscious processes, at the level of behaviour and action we live out such processes everyday all over the world' (2006: 4).

On the positive side of the ledger, psychodynamic theory does encourage an analysis of the affective relationship between the leader and follower. It encourages us to look to our past to identify deeply ingrained and recurrent patterns that might undermine our ability to become a fully effective and responsible leader and follower. It also asks the awkward questions about leadership that might provoke discomfort but nonetheless should not be left unasked. Goethals (2005) approvingly notes that it dares to suggest that perhaps people have a fundamental instinct to follow that is bolstered by a deep-seated 'thirst for obedience'. Perhaps these are fundamental drivers for leadership and, as such, deserve further enquiry.

social identity theory of leadership

The third and final theory which emphasizes the process by which followers construct leaders is called the social identity theory of leadership. It proposes that the extent to which a leader is either selected or accepted by a particular group will depend on how 'prototypical' (i.e. representative) she or he is to that group (van Knippenberg and Hogg, 2003). Hogg defines prototypicality as 'a fuzzy set of features that captures ingroup similarities and intergroup differences regarding beliefs, attitudes, behaviours and feelings' (2005: 56).

It draws upon the popular saying that 'like attracts like'. However, instead of the leader being attracted to a follower who shares a similar background and beliefs, and consequently brings a follower into his or her group, social identity theory highlights the reverse process through which the leader is picked by followers or is chosen to be supported by followers precisely because he or she is most like them. When we talk about 'like' here, we mean how closely the leader represents the group's characteristics as well as its aspirations, values and norms.

Prototypicality is not the only basis for leadership, however. People also rely on general and more task-specific schemas or stereotypes of leadership behaviours which have been dubbed by Robert Lord and his colleagues as 'leader categories' or 'leader schemas' (Lord, 1985). These will be become particularly significant when we move our discussion on to the influence of culture on leadership in Chapter 4.

The importance of these stereotypes we hold about appropriate and inappropriate behaviour diminishes as group prototypicality becomes more important. That is, group membership becomes psychologically more salient. A group is psychologically salient if being part of it is important for someone as a basis for defining who they are, what they believe in, and how they function as an individual. This could be a gang, an Internet discussion group, a sports team, a fan club or a service club. While you might have a general view of what constitutes good or bad leadership, you will put up with leadership behaviour that is at odds with your ideals if belonging to the group is very important to you.

The way social identity theory is set up, the study of leadership begins with the group and not the leader. Assume you are observing a group of people, how does that group go about selecting and supporting an appropriate leader – nominal or otherwise? Social identity theorists suggest that this takes place in three broad phases (Hogg, 2005). First, a group member who is the most prototypical will appear to exercise influence over other group members. Second, because the most prototypical member is consensually liked by the group members (i.e. he or she is socially attractive), this will empower that person and enable him or her to influence other members. Eventually, that person will begin to be imbued with prestige and status. In the final phase of the process, group members begin to attribute the success of their leader to that person's special personality and not because of their prototypicality. In this way a charismatic personality of the leader is constructed (Shamir, 2007).

By the same token, when the leader begins to fail to fully represent the group, to 'sell out' to other interests, followers might decide that this is due to personality defects of the leader. Consequently, they may decide to withdraw their support. In politics this is often the fate of populist leaders who come to power as a result of grassroots movements but, without the support of a political machine, lose the support of their original followers as they attempt to build a broader coalition of support with other groups in order to stand a chance of gaining or maintaining wider power. The spurned in-group may respond by selecting a leader who is more prototypical.

Social identity theory has been empirically tested in both laboratory and naturalistic field settings. For example, one laboratory study asked students to anticipate joining a group in order to discuss university resource allocation for undergraduate classes (Hogg et al., 2001). The salience of belonging to a particular group was manipulated in such a way as to make membership seem more or less important to the students. Participants were informed that their group was to have either an 'agentic/instrumental' (i.e. male stereotypical) norm or a 'communal/expressive' (i.e. female stereotypical) norm for how the discussion was to be conducted within their groups. Participants were also told that a leader had been randomly appointed – they discovered that the leader was either a male or female. The study found that group salience would increase the perceived effectiveness of male leaders for those groups who had been assigned an agentic/instrumental norm and female leaders of groups with a communal/expressive norm. It would also reduce the perceived effectiveness of male leaders of groups with communal/expressive norms and female leaders of groups with agentic/instrumental norms. In other words, the study found that when dealing with matters that count, leadership effectiveness depends more heavily on the match of the leader to the group prototype.

Social identity theory can be helpful in making sense of a number of contemporary leadership issues. For example, research has shown that in Western societies, demographic minorities (e.g. women and ethnic minorities women) can find it difficult to attain top leadership positions because of what is widely described as a 'glass ceiling' (Stafsudd, 2004). If organizational prototypes (e.g. of speech, dress, attitude, interaction styles) are societally cast so that minorities do not match them well, then minorities are unlikely to be endorsed as leaders under conditions when organizational prototypicality is more important – that is when organizational identification and cohesion are high. This might arise under conditions of uncertainty such as when a company is under threat from a competitor or a potential takeover. This is an unfortunate tendency for a number of reasons, not least because it is often the case that, when a company is in most in need of change, an outsider's perspective is what is most needed to lead the company out of its difficulties.

towards a general model

Each of these three follower-centric theories – the romance of leadership, psychoanalytic and social identity theories – provides a useful insight into the process by which followers construct leadership. Boas Shamir suggests that if they are intertwined we can begin to develop a general model of the construction of leadership by followers. Beginning with the individual, drawing on a number of motivational theories, we need to understand that the follower has several unmet needs which a potential leader may or may not be able to fulfil. These are the need for clarity (e.g. what should we be doing? where are we going?), the need for meaning (e.g. what are we doing this for?) and the need for safety (e.g. will we be OK if we do this?).

Leaders are constructed in light of these unmet needs at the level of the individual and at the social level. Individuals construct leaders through the processes of attribution (e.g. they believe they are responsible for causing certain things); projection (e.g. attributing our ideals, wishes and desires to the leader), transference (e.g. responding to a leader as if they were a significant person from childhood) and idealization (e.g. they can do no wrong). At the societal level leaders are constructed through the twin processes of social information processing and social contagion.

Based on these constructions leaders are selected, supported and their influence is accepted. This is by no means a static process. Construction is work that is always in progress. Leaders are constantly being assessed and compared to other leaders, real or imagined. Likewise, as Mary Uhl-Bien and Rajnandini Pillai (2007) have intriguingly argued, followers and leaders also construct notions of followership. Followers either reinforce or refine their constructions as new information comes to light, via direct or indirect interaction, either with themselves or influential others who report on these interactions. Sometimes, when leaders are seen to fail in a major way, followers become so disenchanted and angry that they are forced to demolish their constructions and seek an alternative leader. Because most of these theories have been preoccupied with explicating how leaders are created, the processes by which leaders are deconstructed, or if you like 'de-created', are relatively unexplored.

Follower-centric theories have sought to turn a lot of the conventional leader-centric research that was discussed in Chapter 2 on its head. They have shown that there is indeed much to be gained by starting our study of leadership with the follower and not the leader. In this regard they have provided a much-needed correction and counterbalance to the dominant preoccupations of leadership scholars. In fact we might even go so far as to ask, given the influence that followers can exert over leaders, why we might not consider the possibility of followers acting as leaders. Indeed why not get rid of the leader–follower dichotomy altogether? It is to this possibility that we now briefly turn.

followers as leaders: shared leadership

This approach is technically neither leader-centred nor follower-centred because it rejects the distinction between leaders and followers. Leadership is seen not as a role, but as a function or an activity that can be shared among members of a group or organization. Fundamentally, at the core of this approach is a belief that followers can and should be given their chance to lead, as it is not only the right thing to do but also the smartest thing to do. Traditional command-and-control, hierarchically-based organizations are seen as being no match for the flat, laterally-integrated network organizations in the context of a rapidly changing competitive global economy.

We can think of the various theories which advocate that followers should act as leaders along a continuum. At the more conservative end of the continuum is the notion of 'co-leadership', which recognizes that leadership is rarely the preserve of one individual but frequently is exercised by a pair of individuals, a 'Number One'/'Number Two' combination such as a CEO and a CFO or a group of individuals such as a top management team (Alvarez and Svejenova, 2005). A good example of this type of leadership would be the triumvirate that collectively lead Google.

Further along the continuum is 'shared leadership': the notion that the responsibility for guiding a group can rotate among its members, depending on the demands of the situation and the particular skills and resources required at that moment. Any member can lead the group for a certain period, during a key phase in a project, and then leadership can be passed on to someone else. For example, Joseph Raelin (2003) in his book, *Creating Leaderful Organizations*, argues with infectious passion that 'in the twenty-first century organization, we need to establish communities where everyone shares the experience of serving as a leader, not sequentially, but concurrently and collectively' (2003: xi). The principal task of senior management in this kind of organizational milieu is to produce the environment and the climate where followers can feel genuinely empowered to lead within and beyond the organization.

Even further along the continuum is the notion of 'distributed leadership' in which the team leads its work collectively by creating norms of behaviour, contribution and performance, and by supporting each other and maintaining the morale of the group (Day, Gronn and Salas, 2004; Gronn, 2002). This perspective complements, but does not replace, the perspective of leadership as an input to team processes and performance. However, a singularly zealous advocate of this approach Jeffrey Nielsen, in his book *The Myth of Leadership*, 'makes the case for the end of leadership as we commonly know it – that is, rank-based management – and introduces a method for developing an organization into a true society of peers. I call this model the peer-based organization' (2004: x).

These theories tend to be more normative rather than descriptive. They talk about how things should be rather than how they necessarily are. However, case studies of exemplary practice are enthusiastically presented from companies as diverse as law firms, car manufacturers and IT service providers as evidence that shared and dispersed leadership are more than a gleam in the organizational theorist's eye. Though still a rarity, these forms of leadership do exist and can succeed.

At the more radical end of the continuum is the notion that the term leadership might be profitably dropped as a useful means of understanding organizational behaviour. Alvesson and Sveningsson (2003), for example, have shown through their empirical study of a research and development company that although senior and middle managers used the term 'leadership' freely to describe all manner of activities that were taking place within their organization, when pressed to expand upon and explain how leadership actually works, they were generally at a loss to do so. In light of this finding, and the general concerns they have about the inconsistency of definitions of leadership coupled with our tendency to romanticize leadership, the authors concluded that perhaps we should seriously question the existence of leadership and, by association, followership as a distinct phenomenon. Instead we might probably be better to think of leadership as a hypothetical construct that has no empirical reality.

Because notions of shared and distributed leadership are attracting so much interest among leadership and organizational scholars as well as practitioners and consultants, we will devote an entire chapter (Chapter 5) to the topic. In that chapter we will also pick up on and expand upon the critically-oriented post-structuralist approaches to leadership that question many of the fundamental assumptions that leadership researchers have made about the existence of leadership as a distinct phenomenon. For now we want to close this chapter with an approach that recognizes the contributions of the follower-centric theories discussed above and seeks to integrate these with considerations of the role of the leader in constructing leadership. Indeed it sees leadership as something that is essentially co-produced by followers and leaders.

followers as co-producers of leadership

The idea that leadership is a relationship based on a mutual exchange between leaders and followers is not new. Hollander (1958) for example, suggested that leadership is a two-way influence and social exchange relationship between leaders and followers. Messick (2005) describes leadership as a mutually beneficial relationship predicated on psychological exchange, in which leaders ideally strive to provide their followers with the following: vision and direction, protection and security, achievement and effectiveness, inclusion and belongingness, and pride and self-respect. Robert Greenleaf (1977) has famously encapsulated the lender's ultimate obligation to her or his followers with the idea that leaders should strive to become 'servant leaders'. In return, followers ideally provide leaders with: focus and self-direction, gratitude and loyalty, commitment and effort, cooperation and sacrifice, and respect and obedience. Of course, it is very rare that all of these needs are either met or even required by both leaders and followers.

It is unusual for there to be an explicit contract between leaders and followers but there may well be some form of an implicit contract. While equilibrium is achieved between followers and leaders, leadership will be sustained. When it begins to become unbalanced, that is, leaders and followers are providing too little and/or taking too much, then the relationship ultimately has to be renegotiated. One of the most celebrated examples of leadership illustrates this principle in dramatic fashion. The leadership produced by Ernest Shackleton and the 28 crew members of the *Endurance* expedition, when their ship was crushed in the ice floes off the coast of Antarctic is held up by many as the apotheosis of leadership and its lessons have been widely imparted throughout boardrooms. At various points in the epic and perilous journey back to civilization, the leadership relationship became strained and occasionally challenged, but the numerous accounts of the voyage have shown how both Shackleton and his followers acted to preserve and strengthen the leadership relationship in the knowledge that this was vital to the survival of the group (Shackleton, 1999).

The best effort to date to model the co-production of leadership in a dynamic way is Leader-Member Exchange (LMX) theory which, based on repeated empirical observation, argues that leader–follower relationships evolve through three distinct phases (Graen and Uhl-Bien, 1995). At the initial 'stranger phase', interactions are largely formal, rule-bound and driven by self-interest rather than the good of the group. Some relationships never evolve from this stage. However, others may progress to a second phase, the 'acquaintance' phase – a testing phase in which the leader gives the follower the opportunity to take on more responsibility in return for inside information, and friendship and support. Assuming both the leader and the follower pass the test, the relationship becomes based more on mutual trust and respect and less on formal contractual obligations. At the final 'mature' phase, there is a high degree of reciprocity between leaders and followers; each affects and is affected by the other. Leaders and followers become tied together in productive ways that go well beyond the traditional hierarchically defined work relationship towards a transformational leadership relationship.

LMX theory is intuitively appealing. It accords with the experiences we have had both as follower and as leader. It brings into relief the fact that differences exist in the quality of relationships that leaders have with individual followers. There are times we have really got on with a boss and there are times when we haven't, and yet others seem to get on famously with that boss. It also issues a cautionary note in warning leaders of the dangers of being selective in whom they choose to favour as this fosters divisive in-groups and out-groups within the larger group. Leaders are, therefore, encouraged to cultivate high-quality exchanges with all of their followers, recognizing that ultimately it always 'takes two to tango'.

Keith Grint has noted that leaders can learn a lot about how to lead from their followers. He draws an intriguing parallel between the challenge of learning how to lead for the first time and the challenge of learning how to become a good parent, noting that 'in both cases, and counter-intuitively, it is the junior that teach their superordinates how to lead' (2005: 104). In order to do this, open, honest and continual feedback is essential. Looking back on how we learned to become parents we probably should have devoted more time and effort to trying to learn from our children instead of relying on more traditional sources such as our parents, our friends or child-rearing books.

The parent–child metaphor, especially in light of our discussion of psychoanalytic theories of leadership, is potentially fraught with complications – not least because of its implicitly paternalistic or maternalistic view of leadership which all leadership scholars worth their salt are trying to rid the world of. However, we think it's helpful here because it addresses the joint responsibility that leaders and followers have to open up lines of communication with each other. We need to create leadership relationships that are based on 'constructive dissent' rather than 'destructive consent' (Bratton, Grint and Nelson, 2004). This is a relationship in which followers are willing and capable of questioning and suggesting alternative courses of action in a way that does not undermine or personally attack the leader, and leaders are open and actively supportive of such efforts.

The movie, *The Queen*, provides a striking example of a highly celebrated moment when the roles between leader and followers were reversed. It is a fictional depiction of the behind-the-scenes turmoil within the Royal Family in the aftermath of Princess Diana's death. The Queen is stoically determined to follow protocol and to mourn the death privately and not bow to her subjects' desire, fanned by the media, for her to publicly acknowledge the death. In the end the Queen acquiesces making a public statement via television and by ordering the Royal Ensign to be flown at half-mast above Buckingham Palace. In dramatically compelling fashion, we witness a liminal moment in which the followers are seen to lead the leader. A sub-plot in the film is, of course, the newly-elected Tony Blair's role in influencing the Queen to change her stance in the interests of preserving the monarchy's leadership in the longer term. One, of course, can't help musing at the end of the film whether Tony Blair himself may have lost sight of the principle of follower-led leadership when he made the decision to take the United Kingdom into the War in Iraq.

Perhaps Tony Blair and other besieged leaders might derive some form of comfort from the lessons that Keith Grint distils in his book, *The Arts of Leadership*. On the surface, this book appears to be yet another conventional celebration of the heroic pursuits of well-known historical figures such as Horatio Nelson and Florence Nightingale, as well as business leaders Freddie Laker and Richard Branson. From these accounts, Grint provides evidence not of their cumulative successes but of the propensity regularly and routinely to fail and make mistakes. What distinguishes them from leaders whom we have long since forgotten is the preponderance of their followers to consistently support and cover up for them. He poignantly concludes, 'the trick of the leader is to develop followers who privately resolve the problems leaders have caused or cannot resolve, but publicly deny their intervention' (2001: 420).

To date we have developed a reasonably robust understanding of the different types of leader, but we still tend to treat followers as a homogeneous entity. Collinson (2006) has noted that studies of leadership need to develop a broader and deeper understanding of followers' identities and the complex ways in which these selves may interact with those of leaders. His post-structuralist approach to studying leadership highlights that followers' identities may be more differentiated and contested within the workplace than is generally assumed. Collinson's own empirical research has shown that leaders are often surprised by the unanticipated way followers react to their plans (Collinson, 2005). Followers are smarter and more cunning than they tend to be given credit for, whether it is in the way they appear to support, conform or resist.

There is a well-worn saying that 'we get the leaders we deserve'. This is a statement that infuriates many of those we lecture to as it runs counter to the prevailing leader-centric wisdom. We believe, however, there is much to be said for this statement as it encourages everybody to take an interest in, and play an active role in producing the highest form of leadership we can. The follower-centred perspectives of leadership are helpful in this regard because, as Shamir notes, they enable us to 'reverse the lens' of leadership; they encourage us as followers to not only look at leaders but also at ourselves and others as followers. In reversing the lens, however, 'it is important to examine not only how followers contribute to the construction of a leadership relationship, but also how they empower the leader and influence his or her behaviour and what is their contribution to determining the consequence of the leadership relationship' (2007: xxi).

conclusion

In this chapter we surveyed wide-ranging work done by those who have been curious about that other generally unheralded group of people when it comes to leadership, namely the followers. We looked at various theories that have conceptualized followers to varying levels of significance, either as moderators or constructors, substitutes, or co-producers of leadership. This work has sought to provide a much needed counterbalance to the predominant lopsided focus on leaders held not only by academics but by the general populace. We believe that this work creates a more holistic and complete picture of how leadership works or fails. Given its youthful and partially formed nature, follower-centred perspectives also provide plenty of scope for producing fresh and exciting new research. Finally, and most importantly, it encourages us to reflect and actively think about what we might change in our much rehearsed role as followers to co-create better and higher forms of leadership.

4

Cultural Perspectives on Leadership

'One of the most important developments in the study of cross-cultural leadership in the past several years has been the recognition that this is a valid and appropriate field of study, rather than simply being seen as an adjunct to cross-cultural research, or to leadership research'.

Marcus Dickson, Deanne Den Hartog and Jacqueline Mitchelson (2003: 748)

introducing context into leadership

In the previous two chapters we focused initially on the leader's role in creating leadership and then, to counterbalance this view, we looked at various efforts to understand and explain the role of the follower. We concluded at the end of Chapter 3 that it was more useful to think of leadership as something that is co-produced by leaders and followers, not losing sight of the asymmetrical power relationship that exists between them. We also recognized that leadership is something that is co-produced within a specific context.

The *Collins English Dictionary* defines 'context' in two ways. First, 'as the parts of a piece of writing, speech, etc., that precede and follow a word or passage and contribute to its full meaning'. Second, as 'the conditions and circumstances that are relevant to an event, fact, etc.'. It derives from the Latin noun 'contextus' meaning a putting together and the verb 'contexere', meaning to weave, to braid. These are both useful and complementary ways of thinking about how context influences leadership.

Leadership does not occur in a vacuum. The place where and the time in which leadership is created influences how the leaders and followers go about co-producing leadership. It also affects why it is done and for what purposes. Think about how you would approach leading a student protest compared to leading a memorial service for a family member. As Osborn et al. argue, 'leadership is embedded in the context. It is socially constructed in and from a context where patterns over time must be considered and where history matters' (2002: 798). How we have led in the past influences how we lead today and tomorrow. In effect, by bringing context into the analysis we are suggesting that the 'when?' and 'where?' questions should be given a lot more prominence when we study leadership.

This is by no means a one-way process. In fact, as we saw in Chapter 2, a key task of leadership is to define the situation or context for the group in such a way that it motivates the group to pursue a certain goal. The 'management of meaning' as it is often referred to is the process by which leaders endeavour to align their interpretation of the situation (commonly called a 'frame') with their followers' (Bolman and Deal, 1997). The Shackleton example discussed in the previous chapter graphically illustrates this point. Other expeditionary groups may have decided that having your ship crushed in Antarctic ice floes was reasonably sound grounds for accepting that the situation was hopeless. Through good leadership the expedition was able to define it as an extremely difficult but hopeful situation.

As we saw in Chapter 3, situational and contingency leadership theorists have acknowledged context albeit in a partial way by building various independent variables into the leadership equation. In general however, as Lyman Porter and Grace McLaughlin (2006) have concluded from their review of leadership research, context, like the weather, is talked about in polite conversation but rarely studied systematically. One of the reasons for this is that context is considerably tougher to pin down: it's invariably intangible yet all-encompassing and very difficult to measure. By contrast, it's much easier and more enticing to stick with real, live people such as leaders and followers.

Those researchers who have highlighted organizational context in their leadership studies tend to acknowledge seven influential components: the goals/purpose of the organization (e.g. its strategy and mission); the composition of its people (e.g. its demographics and its capabilities); the organization's core processes (e.g. its technologies, policies and governance model); the state/condition of the organization (e.g. how successful it is); time (e.g. what stage it is at in its organizational lifecycle); its structure (e.g. size, hierarchy, degree of centralization, and spatial distance) and finally, its culture/climate (e.g. its norms, values and ethics).

Culture and structure have received the lion's share of the attention from researchers as the most significant contextual influences on leadership. In this chapter we will focus our attention on culture. We will be looking at structure in the following chapter when we examine various ways in which organizational structure has or should be modified in order to promote an environment in which leadership becomes increasingly dispersed and distributed throughout the entire organization.

culture and leadership

In Chapter 1, we noted that defining leadership is an activity that is fraught with peril. In bringing culture and leadership together we are effectively asking for trouble as culture has been defined, debated and disputed to an even greater extent than leadership. As Mats Alvesson has wryly observed, 'culture is rather like a black hole: the closer you get to it the less light there is thrown on the topic and the less chance you have of surviving the experience' (1993: 3). This dire warning aside, we have found the linkage between leadership and culture to be one of the most intellectually satisfying areas to explore. It is also an area that the practitioners we work with find endlessly fascinating.

Leadership is essentially a cultural activity – it is suffused with values, beliefs, language, rituals and artefacts. Whether we look at a chief executive giving a speech at an Annual General Meeting or two rival gangs meeting to dispute the boundary of their home ranges, culture mediates the ways in which a group of individuals come together to enact leadership. In light of this, it is surprising to learn that a great deal of leadership research either ignores or downplays the cultural dimension in favour of psychological and sociological dimensions.

The most vocal champion of culture and leadership has been Geert Hofstede, a Dutch academic whose work has attracted in equal parts admiration and critique. Hofstede defines culture as 'the collective programming of the mind which distinguishes the members of one group or category from another' (1991: 5). He notes that culture is something that is learned not inherited. It lies somewhere between an individual's unique personality and human nature and is likened to the 'software of the mind'. Hofstede identifies several layers of culture in which the collective mental programming activities operate. At the inner core is the organization in which you work. The outer layer is the country or countries that you live or have lived in. The layers in between these two extremes include your social class, your generation, your gender as well as your regional and/or ethnic and/or religious and/or linguistic affiliation. With respect to looking at the relationship between culture and leadership, most leadership researchers have been preoccupied by the organizational and national layers of culture.

leadership and organizational culture

At a very simplistic level, organizational culture can be understood as 'the way we do things around here' (Deal and Kennedy, 1982). Its importance becomes perhaps most apparent to us when we are endeavouring to become a member of a group, such as when we start a new job. Somewhat ironically, however, we are invariably able to make the most sense of an organization's culture once we have left it and joined another organization.

Edgar Schein, the most influential thinker in the area of organizational culture has more formally defined culture as:

> A pattern of basic assumptions that a given group has invented, discovered, or developed in learning to cope with its problems of external adaptation and internal integration, and that have worked well enough to be considered valid and, therefore, to be taught to new members as the correct way to perceive, think and feel in relation to these problems. (Schein, 2004: 9)

According to Schein, a key function of leadership is the creation, management and sometimes even the destruction of organizational culture. Leaders do this through what he describes as primary 'culture embedding' mechanisms such as role modelling; what they pay attention to, measure and resource; how they react to crises; and who they select, promote and reward within the organization. Schein also describes secondary mechanisms that leaders can work with in creating organizational culture. These include such things as organizational design and structure; the stories, legends and myths they promulgate; rites and rituals (such as retirement and Christmas parties); the layout of the physical space in which employees work; and Dilbert's favourite perennial targets for ridicule: mission and vision statements. As the familiar cliché suggests, because 'actions speak louder than words' the secondary mechanisms which many managers associate with 'culture-building' activities are all for nought if they are inconsistent with the easily taken-for-granted primary mechanisms.

Inspired by Schein's thinking and that of other management gurus' – and egged on by legions of consultants – managers wholeheartedly embraced the idea of organizational culture during the 1980s to the point where you were nobody unless you were working on creating a dynamic and innovative corporate culture. Practitioners tended to see culture as something that the whole organization 'had'. It was either a good or a bad culture and it had to be properly managed, from the chief executive all the way down to the shop floor (Huczynski and Buchanan, 2006). In this regard, the interest in corporate culture closely paralleled the dramatic rise in interest in transformational and charismatic leadership described in Chapter 2.

Academics, on the other hand, took a more circumspect view. They tended to think of organizational culture as something that was always in the process of being created, not exclusively by leaders but by everybody concerned with the organization. Moreover, it was perhaps naïve to think of the organization as having a single unitary culture with everybody pulling feverishly together in the same direction. Organizations were more likely to be either pluralistic in nature, made up of a number of loosely linked sub-cultures, or highly fragmented in that they were always in a state of flux with transitory sub-groups coming together around specific issues, actively in conflict with each other (Martin, 1993).

Many academics (as well as employees) also took issue with the use of culture as just another means of exerting managerial control. While on the surface it was a kinder, gentler and more palatable control mechanism, the demands it made of employees – especially those working in 'high-commitment' organizations – were excessive and potentially immoral. The use of corporate culture as a form of normative control, especially among the professional staff, is illustrated to chilling effect in Gideon Kunda's ethnographic study of an IT company called 'Tech' located in the Silicon Valley (Kunda, 1992). In addition to the sinister effects of leading and managing through corporate culture, others have argued that, ultimately, it is an exercise in futility. As one commentator noted, 'most anthropologists would find the idea that leaders create culture preposterous: leaders do not create culture; it emerges from the collective social interaction of groups and communities' (Meek, 1988: 459).

While the reservations listed above about the limitations and dangers associated with leaders endeavouring to create and shape organizational cultures are well taken, we cannot ignore – nor should we – the powerful influence that an organization's founder can exert on the dominant culture of an organization for good or bad. Following Schein's symbolic-functionalist line, if what the founder proposes attracts sufficient support from followers both within and outside the organization and is seen to work over the long term, then those values and assumptions will gradually become shared by the organization. They will also persist long after the founder has moved on.

Organizational culture is a remarkably resilient phenomenon. This becomes readily apparent when you try to lead change within it. This is one of the reasons why the first thing Brad does when he joins an organization is to track down a copy of its history. While these tomes do not tend to make for the most gripping reading material, you will be amazed how instructive they can be in explaining the present-day culture that permeates the place.

In one of our earlier books called the *The Hero Manager,* in which we featured nine of New Zealand's most successful chief executives, we were struck by just how much cultural leadership the founders were able to exert over their organizations when compared to those who had succeeded other chief executives (Jackson and Parry, 2001). Dick Hubbard, the founder of Hubbard's Foods, a cereal maker within New Zealand, is prototypical in this regard. Customers buy his company's cereal, for his well-known stand on corporate social responsibility as much as for its nutritional value. Needless to say, Dick has had a considerably tougher time exerting the same kind of influence in his new role as the Mayor of Auckland, the country's notoriously fractious council.

Interest in organizational culture reached its zenith during the mid-part of the 1990s. As Ian Palmer and Cynthia Hardy conclude, for academics it is now 'dead, dominant and deconstructed'; whereas for practitioners it is a 'double-edged sword' that must be wielded with due care and attention (Palmer and Hardy, 2001). Initially held up as an antidote to the predominantly normative, functionalist and quantitative research that was being carried out on organizations, organizational culture provided a means to explore the 'soft side' of management and leadership. Culture has been subsequently absorbed into the mainstream. It is now firmly entrenched in the corporate lexicon and continues to generate impressive business for both global and local consultancies ready to provide a cultural audit and cultural rejuvenation programmes, as well as executive coaching for leaders charged with the task of turning around companies with deeply entrenched unhealthy corporate cultures.

With respect to exploring the relationship between leadership and culture, interest has shifted away from organizational culture towards the challenge of leading organizations with operations based in different national contexts. The increasing globalization of trade, finance, production and consumption presents a complex array of business challenges and opportunities which require an unprecedented level of intercultural competence and understanding.

▓▓▓▓ cross-cultural leadership

Cross-cultural leadership refers to leadership in which a leader endeavours to influence the activities and goals of a culturally diverse group by appealing to their systems of shared knowledge and meaning. Cross-cultural leadership recognizes the moderating effect that culture can have on leadership processes. It also seeks to discover the similarities and differences between cultures regarding what is generally considered to constitute appropriate and inappropriate leader–follower relationships.

Interest in cross-cultural leadership was initially prompted by the rapid expansion of a large expatriate workforce driven to the far corners of an increasingly globalized world. These managers often experienced 'culture shock', as they set about trying to adjust their management and leadership styles to a different set of dominant norms and expectations in the host society. The expatriate's need to understand the fundamentals of intercultural interactions, combined with their sponsoring organization's need to successfully manage international assignments, drove the demand for cross-cultural leadership theory and skill development.

In response, a whole new genre of practical management guides has emerged which provide helpful 'laundry lists' of specific cultural do's and don'ts, ranging from how to greet prospective business partners to how to properly conduct lunch. The highly successful *Culture Shock!* series of books is typical with its promise to guide 'the reader through the mindscapes of a country's psyche explaining the do's and don'ts, social customs and traditions, business and social etiquette'. Other books provide colourful case studies from a number of different national contexts which provide cautionary tales of the misunderstanding and transgressions that can occur when managers try to impose their ways of doing things in a foreign land (Hickson and Pugh, 2001; Hooker, 2003).

In one of the best exemplars of this genre, David Thomas and Kerr Inkson argue that in order to survive in an increasingly globalized business environment, managers need to develop their levels of 'cultural intelligence' (Thomas and Inkson, 2004). Cultural intelligence has three components which are linked in a virtuous cycle. First, it requires knowledge of culture and the fundamental principles of cross-cultural interaction that goes beyond etiquette. Second, the culturally intelligent manager needs to practise 'mindfulness', that is, the ability to pay attention in a reflexive and creative way to cues in the cross-cultural situations they encounter. Third, based on this knowledge and mindfulness, the culturally intelligent manager develops a repertoire of behavioural skills which they can draw upon depending on their reading of the situation. The authors suggest that this approach is superior to the 'laundry list' approach to cross-cultural leadership because, in building general as well as specific cultural intelligence, one can face new cultural challenges with increased confidence.

Perceptions of what it means to be a successful 'global leader' are changing. No longer are the 'geocentric globetrotters' who were transferred from country to country to manage foreign operations seen as being the exemplars of good global leadership. For example, Graen and Hui (1999) have argued that all leaders should strive to become 'transcultural creative leaders'. These leaders have the ability to learn how to transcend their childhood acculturation; respect very different cultures; build cross-cultural partnerships based on mutual trust, respect and obligation; actively engage in cross-cultural problem-solving conflicts; and help to construct new cultures based around projects, networks and transitory organizations.

The quest to define a good universal model of global leadership, that is leadership which brings individuals together from diverse national and cultural contexts in a productive and ethical way without any one group dominating, has attracted considerable interest from a number of leadership scholars (Link et al. 2006). This quest has become an urgent one in light of the widespread recognition that global problems – such as global warming, intractable famine, and global epidemics – have outstripped the capacity of existing institutional leadership structures. Good sources for this kind of thinking are the biennial collection of essays published in the *Advances in Global Leadership* series which has just published its fourth volume (Mobley and Weldon, 2006) as well as the Global Leadership Network (www.globalleadership network.net).

cultural influences upon studying leadership

As we observed in the opening chapter, most leadership research has been conducted within the North American context. This creates two problems with respect to the validity and applicability of this research to cultural contexts elsewhere in the world. First, most of the work has been empirically tested within North American contexts. While there is a plethora of diverse cultural contexts within the North American context in which to observe leadership and test leadership theories, it does inevitably constrain the range of potential leadership contexts. To counteract this problem, North American researchers have either consciously sought out different ethnic groups to examine or they have teamed up with researchers from other parts of the world to conduct comparative leadership studies. Attend any management conference and you will come across a variety of papers in which a leadership instrument such as the Multifactor Leadership Questionnaire (MLQ) has been administered in two or more national contexts, and the differences and similarities are presented.

Widening the empirical net does not, however, address a second more profound problem. Namely, that the researchers themselves are products of a specific cultural context. The kinds of questions they tend to ask and the ways they go about answering them are influenced by their immediate cultural milieu. As Hofstede himself has noted, US management and leadership theories tend to focus upon the individual, privilege market processes and, as we saw in the previous chapter, emphasize the manager's needs and perspective at the expense of the employee's. The profound interest shown by American and other Anglo-Saxon countries in leadership is itself a product of historical fascination with heroes and exceptional individuals (Den Hartog and Dickson, 2004). In contrast, European scholars endeavour to situate leadership in a broader social, legal and political context, taking a more critical line towards leaders and a more sceptical view of the desirability, let alone the possibility of leadership.

Having worked in both the European and North American academic contexts and now living in another part of the world, we are conscious of – and indeed endeavour to blend – the valuable insights that both of these academic traditions can bring to the table, even though these scholarly communities tend to talk past rather than with each other. However, living in another part of the world we are also conscious that our understanding of leadership processes is still very geographically limited and skewed towards the West. Certainly, our experience living and working in an explicitly bi-cultural country such New Zealand has exposed us to two quite culturally distinctive models of leadership – the indigenous Maori and the exogenous Pakeha (i.e. non-Maori) models. This has served to spark our interest in, and led us to appreciate the saliency of just how culturally prescribed leadership processes are.

It is important, therefore, to try to become aware and understand the influence that values have in guiding the beliefs, assumptions and behaviours of the leaders we study, but also how these guide what we choose to focus on when we study leadership and how we choose to study it. In the following section we will briefly review some of the key dimensions that have been consistently identified as ways of distinguishing different cultural groups at the societal level.

societal cultural dimensions that influence leadership

Undeniably the most influential global study of cross-cultural leadership is Hofstede's study of 100,000 IBM employees from 49 countries who participated in a survey questionnaire between 1967 and 1973 (Hofstede, 1980). Twenty of the survey's 150 questions were used to create four value dimensions along which Hofstede compared the forty-nine national cultures. Hofstede's work literally launched hundreds of cross-cultural studies which aimed to replicate, extend or refute these sessions and to use these dimensions as the basis for comparing leadership differences and similarities. Den Hartog and Dickson (2004) identify in their excellent overview of leadership and culture, six dimensions – four proposed by Hofstede and two by others – that have been the most commonly proposed and studied.

Hofstedian dimensions

individualism/collectivism

According to Hofstede (1980) cultures characterized by individualism are closely knit social frameworks in which people are supposed to take care of themselves and look after their own interests and those of their close families only. In contrast, collectivist cultures are characterized by a tight social framework in which people distinguish between in-groups and out-groups. In collectivist societies leaders will be expected to keep the good of the in-group uppermost in their minds and will be judged by their ability to protect the group. Followers within individualist societies are more likely to tolerate leaders who look after their own interests and, in fact, are highly prized for their unique achievements.

In a similar vein, Schwartz (1999) has distinguished between societies in which people are expected to be either autonomous or embedded in the group. Autonomy is sought either intellectually through the act of free thought or affectively through the independent pursuit of pleasure. In this regard, leaders would be judged according to the extent to which they are able to provide environments in which followers had a strong sense of belonging and cohesion or were able to encourage their followers to be able to think and express themselves and fulfil their dreams. These two leadership modes were illustrated to dramatic effect in the impromptu and widely celebrated 'kitchen debate' that took place between Richard Nixon and Nikita Khrushchev at the launch of the American National Exhibition held in Moscow in 1959.

hierarchy, status and power distance
Hofstede (1980) defined power distance as the extent to which a society accepted and embraced the fact that power in institutions and organizations is distributed unequally. In cultures with high power distance, authoritarian leadership and a more autocratic decision-making process are more likely to be accepted and expected. In more egalitarian cultures, followers will expect to have a greater say and so will tend to expect an open and more participatory style from their leaders.

In Hofstede's survey, many Latin American countries as well as Asian countries exhibited both high collectivism and high power distance. This is evident in the relatively high respect that Asian students tend to accord their professors compared to Australasian students. The Anglo-Saxon countries, by contrast, were predominantly high in individualism and low in collectivism, along with the Scandinavian/German cluster of countries that exhibited slightly higher levels of collectivism. This difference was evidenced to Brad in the greater appetite that students from the Copenhagen Business School exhibited for group work compared to students from other business schools that Brad has taught at. The Romance countries (e.g. France, Italy, Spain) along with Belgium and South Africa were characterized by high individualism and large power distances.

Another issue related to power and status arises from the question of whether status in a particular society should be based on achievement or ascription (Parsons and Shils, 1951). Achievement-oriented societies tend to accord status based on what people have accomplished. Ascribing cultures confer status on the individual because of their age, seniority or their lineage. Within many of the Pacific Islands we see the tension between ascribed and achievement-oriented norms manifest itself in the frustration that many formally educated younger leaders feel. They are anxious to be given the opportunity to lead so that they can apply their new-found knowledge and skills, yet have to defer to the traditional ascribed leadership of the tribal chiefs and elders.

uncertainty avoidance

This dimension describes a society's reliance on social norms and procedures to alleviate the unpredictability of the future. Leaders in countries with high levels of uncertainty avoidance will endeavour to ameliorate the threat of uncertainty and ambiguity by establishing formal rules, emphasizing their technical expertise, and showing little tolerance for deviant ideas and behaviours. If they wish to bring about change, leaders will have to do it within the existing system. Leaders in societies that are more accepting of uncertainty will, by contrast, have to be more flexible and willing to champion change by violating organizational rules and regulations (Shane, Venkataraman and MacMillan, 1995).

masculinity/femininity

This is the dimension over which Hofstede encountered most criticism because it covers too many topics and because of the semantic confusion it creates by alluding to gender (which is, in turn, a culturally produced construct). He argued that, in 'masculine' societies, the dominant social values stressed the virtues of assertiveness and toughness, and the acquisition of money and material possessions. In 'feminine' societies, by contrast, values such as warm social relationships and quality of life are stressed.

The hero leader archetypes that a country holds up and celebrates will vary according to how masculine or feminine the dominant values are within that society. In more masculine countries such as Japan, Austria, Italy, Mexico, Germany and the United Kingdom heroic leaders will tend to be aggressive, decisive and highly visible. The hero in predominantly feminine cultures will be a lot less visible, seeking consensus and relying more on intuition. We can, therefore, appreciate that Margaret Thatcher and Nelson Mandela are, respectively, archetypal masculine and feminine political leaders.

Other dimensions

linguistic/emotional

Two other means of contrasting dominant societal values also have considerable saliency for the conduct of leadership. The first emphasizes language differences. The second emphasizes the role of emotions. Hall and Hall (1990) distinguish societies which are characterized by 'low context languages' such as the Anglo-Saxon, the German and the Scandinavian societies which emphasize the need to be direct, clear and explicit in communication; and societies with 'high context languages' such as the Japanese, Mediterranean, Latin American and

Arabic societies which are less direct, and more ambiguous and subtle. These are the societies that place a high premium on the ability to skilfully 'manage face' (Ting-Tommey, 1988), though in reality all leaders and followers should show a healthy concern for impression management, wherever they are located. Related to this issue, leaders who are concerned with how they present themselves should heed Trompenaars and Hampden-Turner's (1997) distinction between 'affective societies' in which people are encouraged to show their emotions and 'neutral countries' where people are encourage to keep their emotions in check.

assumptions about human nature

When it comes right down to it, do you believe that most humans are fundamentally good or bad? Brad's grandmother was quite clear on this matter; she thought that everyone was basically decent with the exception of a few rotten apples. Kluckhohn and Strodtbeck (1961) have created a societal dimension to capture this value orientation. At one end of the dimension is the generalized assumption that 'human nature is good'. At the other end is the assumption that 'human nature is bad'. In those societies in which people are seen as being fundamentally good, leaders will rely more on building trust and being fair in influencing their followers. In those societies in which people are considered to be fundamentally flawed, leaders will seek to more closely monitor and directly control their followers.

After the publication of his original study, Hofstede acknowledged the existence of a fifth dimension of culture, which incorporated the distinctive philosophy of Eastern Asia (Hofstede and Bond, 1988). This dimension, which was originally labelled 'Confucian dynamism' but later renamed 'long versus short-term orientation', was found to be particularly significant for the Chinese culture. Long-term orientation cultures, typified by China, see truth as a relative phenomenon, have a pragmatic acceptance of change, and emphasize the value of perseverance, thrift and saving for tomorrow. Societies with short-term orientations on the other hand, such as the Anglo-Saxon countries, place great stock in absolute truth, and have a high concern for normative rationality, quick results and the need to live for today.

control orientation

Another persistent means by which cultures are contrasted by leadership scholars is to look at how societies view their relationship with the outside world. For example, Trompenaars and Hampden-Turner (1997) distinguish between 'internal cultures' and 'external cultures'. The former, typified by the United States, have a dominating and controlling attitude towards nature; the latter societies, typified by Middle Eastern countries, are more at ease with natural shifts and cycles of nature. In a similar vein, Schwartz (1999) describes 'mastery cultures' in which people are encouraged to master change and exploit the environment in order to achieve their goals. In these cultures, leaders need to be dynamic, competitive and strongly oriented towards achievement. Cultures at the opposing pole are labelled 'harmony cultures'. In these cultures, people are encouraged to understand and integrate with their natural environment, rather than change or exploit it. Leaders, therefore, need to take a more holistic view and try to understand the social and environmental implications of organizational actions.

the critique of cultural dimensions

While the Hofstede study has been hugely influential in our thinking about leadership and culture, it has been widely critiqued on several fronts. First, with respect to the design of the study, the research was based entirely on attitude survey questionnaires with too few questions asked of employees from just one company (Tayeb, 1996). Second, not all of the dimensions are well grounded in theory (e.g. masculinity/ femininity and uncertainty avoidance) and several anomalies have been detected (e.g. Trompenaars and Hampden-Turner, 1997). Moreover, after thirty years there are grounds for thinking that these data are now outdated (Mead, 1994). For example, a study of students from 11 European nations using the same dimensions as used by Hofstede revealed a significant convergence of national values, with gender becoming a more significant differentiator than national origin for masculinity, uncertainty avoidance and individualism–collectivism (Gooderham and Nordhaug, 2001).

Osland et al. (2000) have suggested that the Hofstedian framework is best viewed as a form of 'sophisticated stereotyping' because 'it is based on theoretical concepts and lacks the negative attributions often associated with its lower-level counterpart. Nevertheless, it is still limiting in the way it constrains perceptions of behaviour in another culture'. This weakness is made very apparent when we are confronted with 'cultural paradoxes'; that is behaviour exhibited by an individual from a particular culture that violates our conceptions of what we think a particular culture is like. For example, how do we reconcile the fact that, while America is supposed to have one of the most individualist cultures in the world, Americans devote more time and energy to charitable causes than anyone else in the world? Osland and Bird suggest that if we want to become more competent intercultural leaders we need to move beyond this sophisticated stereotyping by developing our abilities as cultural observers, so that we purposely seek out disconfirming evidence that defies our cultural stereotypes.

Along these lines, Kanter and Corn (1994) caution us to avoid the temptation of committing a basic error when analysing cultural behaviour. The 'fundamental attribution error' is the tendency to attribute our own behaviour to a particular situation but the other person's behaviour is attributed to their character. Commenting on research that they conducted of takeovers of American companies by foreign entities, they noted that the significance of cultural differences between employees and managers tended to be overstated. They conclude that:

> 'Cultural values or national differences are used as a convenient explanation for other problems both interpersonal and organizational, such as the failure to respect people, group power and politics, resentment at subordination, poor strategic fit, limited organizational communication, or the absence of problem-solving forums. Such differences are invoked as explanations for the uncomfortable behaviour of others when people have limited contact or knowledge of the context behind the behaviour. In the same way that it is dangerous to ignore the importance of national culture in management, it is just as dangerous to overstate its significance'. (Kanter and Corn 1994: 19)

perceptions of leadership across cultures: the GLOBE study

Another major line of inquiry has sought to identify and delimit the shared prototypes or profiles of outstanding leadership that might be distinctive to specific national cultures. This has been done primarily by examining followers' perceptions of leaders' behaviour, values, attitudes and personality traits (Shaw, 1990), referred to generally as 'implicit leadership theories' (Schyns and Meindl, 2005). As we saw in Chapter 3, prototypes contain a set of attributes that define the essential characteristics of a category, for example, an effective business leader. Leadership categorization theory (Lord and Mayer, 1991) suggests that the better the match between a perceived individual and the leadership concept held by the perceiver, the more likely it is that the perceiver actually 'sees' the individual as a leader. Followers who categorize a manager as a prototypical leader are likely to allow him or her to exert leadership influence on them. If someone looks, acts and sounds like a leader then they must be a leader!

Exploring followers' perceptions of prototypical leaders throughout the world was the central quest of the Global Leadership and Organizational Behaviour Effectiveness research programme, memorably dubbed the 'GLOBE' study (House et al., 2004). The idea for GLOBE came to Robert House in the summer of 1991. Having reviewed a broad array of research into charismatic leadership that had been conducted in a wide range of cultural contexts, he had cause to believe that there might be a basis for believing that charismatic leader behaviour might be universally acceptable and effective. The GLOBE project provided him with the means to ascertain this on a grand scale. The project involved 127 investigators from 62 cultures. Between 1994 and 1997 data were collected from 17,300 middle managers based in a total of 951 organizations. Twenty-seven hypotheses were tested in the study, each linking culture to performance outcomes.

The GLOBE study identified nine major attributes of culture: Future Orientation, Gender Egalitarianism, Assertiveness, Humane Orientation, In-Group Collectivism, Institutional Collectivism, Permanence Orientation, Power Concentration versus Decentralization, and Uncertainty Avoidance. When quantified these attributes are referred to as 'cultural dimensions'. For each of the nine dimensions, items were developed at two levels: societal and organizational. In addition, two measures were used. One tapped the participants' assessment of the extent to which their society or organization engages in certain practices (i.e. as they *are*). The other tapped into their values relating how things *should be* (Den Hartog et al., 1999).

Four of the nine dimensions were identified in Hofstede's landmark study, but were renamed. While the GLOBE project owed a great deal to Hoftstede's work, it was by no means meant to act merely as a big budget remake. As House notes, 'we have a data set to replicate Hofstede's (1980) landmark study and extend that study to test hypotheses relevant to relationships among societal-level variables, organizational practices, and leader attributes and behaviour' (House et al., 2004: xxv).

The GLOBE project also identified six major global leader behaviours. The study found that there is a wide variation in the values and practices relevant to the nine core dimensions of cultures and a wide range of perceptions of what constitutes effective and ineffective leader behaviours. However, in all cultures leader team orientation and the communication of vision, values, and confidence in followers were reported to be highly effective leader behaviours. Perhaps not surprisingly, leadership attributes reflecting irritability, non-cooperativeness, egocentricity, being a loner, ruthlessness and dictatorial attitudes were associated with ineffective leaders. While some variation was found concerning participative leadership, the study found wide variation with respect to two major dimensions of leader behaviour: autonomous leadership and self-protective leadership.

Autonomous leadership is characterized by a high degree of independence from superiors and is reported to contribute slightly toward organizational effectiveness in Eastern European countries (except Hungary) and Germanic Europe countries (except the Netherlands). Self-protective leadership is characterized by self-centredness, status consciousness and narcissism. This type of leadership behaviour is seen to be slightly effective by managers in Albania, Taiwan, Egypt, Iran and Kuwait. These intriguing exceptions aside, one is struck overall by how little variation there appears to be in the ascribed values and practices of effective leaders between managers in the 62 countries surveyed.

The GLOBE project is unquestionably the single most ambitious leadership study to have ever been conducted. It is still, however, very much a work in progress. As the editors of the first book humbly conclude, 'the wealth of findings provided in this book set the stage for a more sophisticated and complex set of questions' (House et al., 2004: 726). They acknowledge that, although the GLOBE findings have identified the various attributes of leadership, they have not identified the behavioural manifestations of such attributes. For example, it is clear from the study that integrity is a universally desirable attribute for leadership, but does it mean the same thing to a Chinese employee as it does to an American one?

The critics of the GLOBE study have also not been idle. Den Hartog and Dickson (2004) note several areas in which this and other pan-national studies have been questioned. For example, the potential for this work to commit an 'ecological fallacy' has been raised. This is the tendency to ascribe what has been noted at one level (e.g. society) to another level of analysis (e.g. the individual). While the GLOBE participants actively endeavoured to address the 'levels of analysis' problem, a series of essays in the October 2006 issue of *Leadership Quarterly* showed that the study's measurement metrics and levels of analysis are still being actively debated (Dickson et al., 2006; Peterson and Castro, 2006; Hanges and Dickson, 2006; Dansereau and Yammarino, 2006). Related to this is the problem of adequate sampling. In large, multicultural countries such as India, China and the United States, it is a daunting challenge to decide which sample would be the most representative.

Another fundamental problem associated with this type of cross-cultural survey is one of translation. How do we ensure that the respondents are interpreting the questions similarly? Even when we provide re-translating checks and balances, we still have to be alert to cultural norms regarding the completion of questionnaires. Anne-Will Harzing (2006) notes that responses to survey questions are influenced by the content of the question and the response style – which is the tendency to respond to questionnaire items regardless of item content. These response styles include acquiesence (ARS), middle response styles (MRS) and extreme response styles (ERS). For example, Hispanics and African-Americans show higher ERS and ARS when compared to European Americans. On the other hand, Japanese/Koreans show lower ERS and higher MRS than US Americans.

The GLOBE project represents a bold and ambitious step towards broadening the empirical net of leadership research but its theoretical base is still firmly rooted in American soil. We gain a great deal in methodological rigour but lose something in philosophical acuity. House's intentions are unquestionably honourable when he states, 'Hopefully, GLOBE will be able to liberate organizational behaviour from the US hegemony' (2004: xxv). However, we feel that, somewhat perversely, American supremacy in this field is strengthened by this project, not challenged.

towards a more cultured understanding of leadership

One of the most accomplished cross-cultural leadership researchers over the past twenty years, Peter Dorfman, has delineated four important caveats that he argues leadership researchers need to consider when applying a cross-cultural lens to leadership research (Dorfman, 2003). The first caveat is to not ignore significant differences within a country or culture, as well as significant differences between countries that are considered part of a country cluster. Along these lines, Brad has been engaged in a research project in New Zealand that has used the GLOBE dimensions to highlight significant differences as well as similarities in the way the indigenous Maori and the exogenous Pakeha people perceive what constitutes outstanding leadership (Pfeifer, Love and Jackson, 2006).

The second caveat Dorfman presents is that expression of a cultural dimension within a culture may vary and seem contradictory at times. For example, how is it possible for followers to value in their leaders both humane and self-protecting behaviour? The third caveat is that individual differences will still exist in the adherence to cultural values and, as such, not all individuals will display the cultural values of their indigenous culture. Thankfully the world is richly populated with nonconformists who either quietly or spectacularly defy their native culture's norms and expectations. *Vive la différence.*

The final caveat – and the one we think is most crucial for leadership researchers to consider – is that 'cultures are not static; they are dynamic and continually evolving'. In order to do this, Eric Guthey

(2005) has observed that leadership and management researchers need to cross what he describes as the 'great divide' and address the occasional antagonisms between humanities-based cultural research, on the one hand, and cultural research rooted in the social sciences, such as the GLOBE project, that has predominated in business schools.

Humanities-based perspectives help us to recognize that culture is all pervasive and consists of all the forms through which people make sense of their lives and works – from opera to pop music to work organizations, leisure pursuits and the home. Each culture is not a separate domain, like economics and politics, as all human contact is culturally mediated. It may be funny, bizarre, disgusting and so on, but it can be understood only in its own context and on its own terms. Cultures are not discrete. We shift from one 'culture' to another. Cultures themselves change all the time through their own momentum and contact, through individual participants, with other cultures. Cultures are constructed by social groups. They are imagined through myths and folklore, manipulated by competing power elements and mobilized for particular ends. Humanities-based perspectives replace an 'essentialist' view of culture with a social constructionist conception of culture which stresses and values plurality, process and politics (Søderberg and Holden, 2002).

We will close this chapter by reviewing five recent studies that provide promising exemplars of how humanities-based leadership research can enrich our understanding of the relationship between culture and leadership. Each of these studies takes an 'emic' approach in that they endeavour to understand the culture from *within* the culture they are studying (Triandis, 1980). Most of the studies we have reviewed in this chapter have been predominantly 'etic' in their approach. That is, they attempt to generalize leadership theory by looking at cultures from outside the ones they are studying.

The first study by Andrew Jones advocates an 'anthropology of leadership' (Jones, 2005). Such an approach studies organizational leadership empirically at the conjunction between local culture schema and larger economic and cultural forces. Based on his ethnographic and documentary research of three companies based in the American South, Jones concluded that one of the key roles of the company's leaders was to be leaders and protectors of 'Southern' culture or, as he evocatively describes them, 'keepers of the tribe'. The leaders derive their influence from 'cultural capital' as authentic locals who grew up in the South combined with their 'managerial capital' as global businessmen derived from gaining MBAs elsewhere and global travel. His 'cultural theory of leadership' suggests that leaders can derive their leadership legitimacy and power from being 'local' and 'global' at the same time.

Using culture as a strategic symbolic resource is not only something that is confined to senior managers, however. An ethnographic study of Israeli employees at a high-tech corporation shows how the employees drew on the distinctiveness of their Israeli national identity to resist a merger between their company and an American company; the two were previously competing international organizations (Ailon-Souday and Kunda, 2003). In an ironic twist, the Israelis used Hofstede-inspired cross-national frameworks in defence against efforts on the part of American managers to integrate the company's management policies and practices.

A further irony is noted by Linda Sue Warner and Keith Grint that, despite most of the leading texts on leadership being American, these texts are virtually silent on the leadership dynamics of the 500 or so federally recognized American Indian tribes who reside there (Warner and Grint, 2006). They note significant differences exist between American Indian and Western approaches to perspectives on leadership. American Indian leadership has often been interpreted by non-indigenous observers as an inability to lead rather than a different ability to lead. Western approaches are often limited to positional approaches, whereas Indian models are more concerned with persuading others to do something that they would not otherwise have done, not on the basis of position but by other means. Western approaches are more concerned with the individual leader. American Indian models are more concerned with how different forms of leadership in different circumstance can serve the community rather than enhance the rewards and reputation of the leader.

Indigenous leadership research is not just a matter of different forms of leadership, it's also about how we go about trying to know it. Indigenous research, like indigenous leadership, requires taking time for discussion, developing consensus, and asking elders and spiritual advisers for consultation and guidance (Christensen, 1991). In New Zealand, Maori intellectuals are developing a distinctively Maori research paradigm which is called 'Kaupapa Maori' in resistance to a Eurocentric colonial heritage and hegemony (Henry and Pene, 2001). Kaupapa Maori literally means the Maori ways of doing, being and thinking, encapsulated in a Maori world-view or cosmology. Kaupapa Maori research, together with research conducted within other Asia-Pacific traditions, not only challenges Western research paradigms, it also critically examines the role of the academy as an implicitly Western institutional form that systematically excludes or marginalizes other ways of knowing.

Adding further fuel to this fire, Lesley Prince argues that, the reasons why leadership remains a tantalizing enigma for Western thinkers and practitioners is the result of two interrelated presuppositions. First, our conceptions of leadership are located in a cultural framework of hierarchy and control that emphasizes outside direction and separation. Second, Western language codes leadership as a noun and, therefore, views it as a separate object of study. By contrast Eastern thought, notably Taoism and Zen, presents a view of leadership, and more especially the use of power, as a fluid set of interrelations coordinated with and within a natural order that is outside our immediate control but of which we are an intimate part.

Whereas for Western thinkers, leadership is about actively taking control, for Taoists it is about engagement and accommodation with circumstances as they are. Prince concludes that:

> the difference in emphasis embodied by Taoism may be helpful in our attempts to understand leadership by moving away from codes, prescriptions and specifications much more towards a located and responsive social skill developed through doing rather than thinking – and emphasis on internal 'knowing' and experience rather than on external instruction. (2005: 106)

Using a striking metaphor, she provocatively invites Western leadership researchers to stop trying to eat the 'menu' of leadership and get on with eating the 'dinner'.

In Chapter 5 we will continue to consider more examples of this type of culturally reflexive and critically oriented emic approach to studying leadership. Based on this emergent critique, we will examine various alternative models of shared, dispersed and distributed leadership that have been put forward in an effort to challenge and replace the top-down heroic models of leadership that have dominated Western thinking and practice.

conclusion

In this chapter we highlighted the role of context in creating leadership, most particularly the influence of culture in enabling and constraining various forms of leadership. The relationship between culture and leadership has been investigated in the context of the organization, with a view towards improving organizational performance by leading and managing the organization's culture. Assuming that an organization can be said to possess a distinct and unitary culture, a number of academics have expressed doubts about the real influence that leaders can or should exert on forming – let alone changing – culture.

The other major thrust has been in understanding societal variations in culture, and the influence these have on desired and actual leadership values and behaviour. The relatively new yet growing field of cross-cultural leadership seeks to help managers to become more effective leaders within and between the diverse cultural contexts they inhabit in an increasingly globalized business environment. The growing interest in leadership research throughout the rest of the world has revealed contributions as well as limitations in the applicability and relevance of the predominantly American-based research to other national and local contexts. Others have argued that it is not just the specificity of the cultures being explored but the culturally specific way in which they have been explored that has limited our ability to understand the full range and depth of leadership practices throughout the world. We, therefore, look forward to more emically-oriented leadership research to complement the preponderance of etically-oriented research within the field of cross-cultural leadership.

5

Critical Perspectives on Leadership

'Concertive control evolved from the value consensus of the company's team workers to a system of normative rules that became increasingly rationalized. Contrary to some proponents of such systems, concertive control did not free these workers from Weber's iron cage of rational control. Instead, the concertive system, as it became manifest in this case, appeared to draw the iron cage tighter and to constrain the organization's members more powerfully'.

J.R. Barker, 1993: 408

So far, we have developed a focus on the leader, then on the followers, and then on the cultural differences between different societies of leaders and followers. Now, we need to examine leadership as the 'glue' that holds all these people together within those 'societies'. The literatures that we will cover are co-leadership, distributed leadership, leaderless workgroups, and team leadership. These are critical perspectives because they challenge the traditional orthodoxies of leadership and following. They challenge the hegemonic view that leaders are the people in charge and followers are the people who are influenced. The critical perspectives make the claim that leadership is a process that goes on between all people and that all people can be involved in leadership, almost in spite of their formal position.

co-leadership

Co-leadership, a concept first coined by Heenan and Bennis (1999) in their book *Co-leaders: The Power of Great Partnerships*, is described as two (or more) leaders in vertically contiguous positions who share the responsibilities of leadership. Brad Jackson, Dale Pfeifer and Bernadette Vine (2006) studied the co-leadership phenomenon by focusing on four leaders in one organization, who were regarded by others as being transformational. With the use of discourse analysis, they explored an interaction between the four leaders and their followers for evidence of both co-leadership and of the communication behaviour that Berson and Avolio (2004) associate with transformational leadership, namely careful listening, careful transmitting, and open communication. 'Careful listener' and 'careful transmitter' are not terms or constructs we would normally use, especially where they imply a sender–receiver or transmission model of communication (which we challenge). Instead, their aim was to explore these communication styles in the authentic communication of transformational leaders. The use of discourse analysis allowed them to explore a real workplace interaction rather than just relying on what people report occurs. Leaders lead through what they say and what they do, so studying the words of those leaders – their discourse – enables researchers to examine how the people *do* their leadership.

One major concern is most studies' focus on a pair of individuals (a leader and a follower), otherwise known as a dyad. In response, many contemporary scholars adopt a critical perspective by examining a leader's influence over a group of multiple followers/organizational processes. However, as signalled by the currently popular shared leadership paradigm, focusing on multiple leaders may also be important. Also of concern is that leadership studies define a generic set of leader behaviours and their effect on followers, but fall short of clearly identifying exactly what those behaviours are. As Alvarez and Svejenova suggest when referring to the wider field, leadership studies 'mostly focus on the personal characteristics and psychology of executives rather than on their actual behaviour and their activities in performing the tasks prescribed by their roles' (2005: 3). They go on to suggest studies of leadership are too often lacking in context. This call is echoed by numerous scholars advocating that we need to determine a better understanding of precisely how leadership manifests in specific contexts, to give a deeper understanding of how leaders' behaviour impacts on the leadership process.

There is a growing debate within leadership studies over whether or not leadership should be regarded either as an individual or a shared activity. When suggesting that leadership is a shared or group-level activity, an individual might step forward to lead or step back to follow depending on the moment and the skills and knowledge required (Pearce and Conger, 2003). Fletcher and Käufer (2003) have noted that shared approaches to leadership question the individual level perspective, arguing that it focuses excessively on top leaders and says little about informal leadership or larger situational factors.

shared transformational leadership

We believe that co-leadership makes an important contribution to the leadership literature, although it currently lacks empirical analysis. Transformational leadership, on the other hand, has gained widespread attention and significant validation, as we have explained. Not that we are intentionally over-emphasizing transformational leadership, but several influential leadership scholars have made references to transformational leadership as a shared process. Burns (1978), widely regarded as the father of transformational leadership, wrote of the existence of *webs* of potential collective leadership. He suggested that individual leaders are likely to merge with others in a series of participant interactions that will constitute collective leadership. In his work on transformational leadership in teams, Bass (1998) notes that transformational leadership could be shared among the team members. However, substitutes for leadership may evolve that help support the team's higher levels of achievement. Additionally, Avolio and Bass (1995) argued that transformational leadership theory can be considered as a multi-level construct and the type of individualized relationship that a leader builds with each follower can also emerge among team members. Hence, the notion of the co-leadership of transformational leadership has been around for a long time. It just has not figured prominently on research agendas.

Kellerman and Webster have cautioned however that 'The prevailing scholarly winds have now shifted so much in favour of collaboration – in contrast to hierarchical decision-making and organizational structures – that the challenge for researchers has become one of guarding against excess' (2001: 493). We must be careful not to overestimate the degree to which transformational leadership is shared between members of a team (Locke, 2003). What we argue here is a special case of shared leadership that acknowledges the importance of both hierarchical authority and collaboration. This is important because, as Kellerman and Webster suggest, collaborative leadership between team members is not necessary – and does not necessarily work – in all circumstances. However, to counter this, evidence suggests that groups make better decisions than individuals (Elkin, Jackson and Inkson, 2004). What we have noted is that leaders often do collaborate, but not with all organizational members. Instead they collaborate with their closet allies, who also usually hold leadership positions within the organization. As always, the consensus is lacking, and the jury is still out. As well as providing a definition for co-leadership, Heenan and Bennis describe co-leaders as 'truly exceptional deputies – extremely talented men and women, often more capable than their more highly acclaimed superiors' (1999: 6). CEO–COO–CFO, president–vice-president, chancellor–vice-chancellor, prime minister–deputy prime minister, and managing director–artistic director are among the leadership partnerships or top management teams featured by many organizations, explicitly dividing leadership roles between more than one leader at the top of an organization. These structures, in executive suites, political organizations and public institutions, give traction to the argument that leadership is often engaged in by more than one leader.

Heenan and Bennis also suggest that we seem to continue to be mesmerized by celebrity and preoccupied with being 'Number 1'. However this belief overvalues the contribution of the general or CEO or president and depreciates the contributions of subordinates. 'The genius of our age is truly collaborative,' they write. 'The shrewd leaders of the future are those who recognize the significance of creating alliances with others whose fates are correlated with their own' (Heenan and Bennis, 1999: viii). Whether it is Geoff Dixon and Margaret Jackson at Qantas, or Theresa Gattung and Roderick Deane at Telecom, we have seen many examples of how the combination of the CEO and the Chairman of the Board makes a better leadership team than just the sum of their two characters.

When things go very well for a publicly-listed company, the CEO gets the leadership kudos and financial reward, and rightly so. The CEO will often pay homage to the support of the Chairman in those dark hours when insecurity or doubt starts to creep in. Similarly, when happily reporting to shareholders at annual general meetings, the Chairman will invariably pay homage to the dedication and leadership of the CEO. Indeed, this co-leadership occurs much more than we, the public, see in the media. We see it occasionally in the business pages of the newspapers and business shows on television, but in reality this co-leadership dynamic is constant and unrelenting. It has to be.

By contrast, corporate failure often correlates with a breakdown in that relationship between CEO and Chairman. We have seen many times in our research that when CEO and Chairman lose sight of their shared destiny, then leadership of the company falters, and company performance is damaged irreparably. In still other case studies, CEOs have confided to us in quiet moments that the relationship between CEO and the union leader are critical to the success or failure of the organization. Granted, this particular example of co-leadership is less relevant in New Zealand and the USA than in the UK or Australia and many other countries. However, the point is well made that co-leadership takes on many and varied guises. When it comes to leadership, an old cliché may well ring true: 'two heads are better than one'.

Although co-leadership has yet to undergo rigorous testing, several scholars suggest that it improves leadership effectiveness (Heenan and Bennis, 1999; O'Toole et al., 2003; Sally, 2002; Alvarez and Svejenova, 2005). Upper Echelons Theory, conceived by Hambrick and Mason (1984) give us some insight into why this might be. This theory suggests that leadership is an important ingredient of organizational perform- ance; however, the complexity of organizations makes it improbable that one leader alone will be able to exert great influence over all mem- bers of the organization. A co-leadership structure makes this more likely, helping to fill the gap between the top-tier leader and the rest of the organization.

Hambrick also argues that strategic leadership occurs in an environ- ment embedded in ambiguity, complexity, and informational over- load. An important responsibility of top-level organizational leaders is enabling the organization to adapt to this complex environment (Boal and Hooijberg, 2000). The skills required successfully to negotiate this increasingly complex environment are extensive and may be too broad to be possessed by one leader (Storey, 2004; Alvarez and Svejenova, 2005). Moreover, collaboration at the senior leadership level improves the success of the strategic organizational partnership (Huxham and Vangen, 2000), allowing top corporate managers adequate time to pay attention to different aspects of the leadership task including day-to- day operational activities and long-term strategy.

Ken had an idea along these lines when he took up the position as Founding Director of the Centre for the Study of Leadership. This co-leadership idea was milling around in his mind when he addressed senior public servants at a conference in Wellington one morning. The topic was CEO succession. He knew that every person has particular expertise at certain aspects of leadership. For instance, one CEO candi- date might be best at the inspirational communication; another might be best at thinking outside the square and fostering innovative thinking. Yet another potential CEO might be best at complex analysis and prob- lem solving. He proposed that perhaps the time had come for multiple CEOs. He regretted saying it, even as the words were leaving his mouth. The resulting astonishment and scepticism from the audience was palpable. Thankfully one bureaucrat said out aloud that he just could not see how the notion of multiple CEOs could work. This comment gave Ken the welcome opportunity to back-pedal quickly and admit that he was just putting ideas out there for debate and that he was not formally making this a strategy that the public sector could adopt. Anyway, he thinks he got out of it. The point is that he now realizes that he was mulling over the notion of co-leadership. This notion has a long way to go, and will be a fertile area for research for years to come. As this discussion suggests, we believe that further scholarly exploration of co-leadership is important for gaining a deeper understanding of the transformational leadership phenomenon.

distributed leadership

Distributed leadership is also refereed to as 'dispersed' leadership. The terms vary slightly, but in effect are saying much the same thing. What this body of literature is dealing with is a departure from the notion that leadership and followership reside within clearly distinguishable persons. Instead, the notion is that leadership – like power and like information – can be moved between people at differing levels of the organizational or societal hierarchy.

Parry and Bryman (2006) have identified five strands to the writing on distributed leadership. First, Manz and Sims (1991) and Sims and Lorenzi (1992) developed an approach which specifies the advantages of a type of leadership that was expected to supersede the 'visionary hero' image of leadership. They developed the ideas of SuperLeadership and Self Leadership. One feature of SuperLeadership is the quaint eccentricity that it is always written as one word with a large L in the middle. A keynote feature, however, is the emphasis that is placed on 'leading others to lead themselves', or at least to demonstrate more leadership themselves. 'Self-leaders' are those people who act on their own through self-discipline and self-behaviour-modification. They are high on the attributes of self-awareness and self-consciousness. These are allied concepts and both are associated with the manifestation of effective leadership. Self-awareness involves the extent to which an individual's attention may be focused internally on certain aspects of oneself. It involves having knowledge (and awareness) of self, including knowledge of one's interest, aptitudes and limitations, including leadership ability, logically. Self-consciousness is a more acute sense of self-awareness, often pre-empted by the attention of others. Indeed, it involves the additional realization that others are similarly aware of you.

Second, Kouzes and Posner (1998) argue that credible leaders develop capacity in others, and have the capacity to turn their 'constituents' into leaders. Bass and Avolio (1990) have referred to 'constituents' as 'associates'; other terms are 'co-workers' or, simply, 'followers'. The great Boas Shamir, speaking at the annual leadership conference at Lancaster University in late 2005, suggested that we think of followers as 'co-producers' rather than 'recipients' of leadership. He also reaffirmed that we should be looking at what is 'going on' between people in terms of leadership, rather than adhering to either a 'leader-centric' or a 'follower-centric' dichotomy. Whichever way we articulate it, quite simply, it is all about the other people you work and interact with. For Kouzes and Posner, the issue is not one of handing down leadership to these other people, but of liberating them so that they can use their abilities to lead themselves and others. Ken's research has supported this proposition (Parry and Proctor-Thomson, 2003). Leadership capability is inherent within many of us and, indeed, can be trained (Parry and Sinha, 2005). However, the crucial issue is that the organizational systems must be made less bureaucratic in order to free, or liberate that leadership potential. One acronym that executives use is RAMPP – reports, approvals, meetings, policies, procedures. If RAMPP is minimized, then the leadership that is inherent within all workers can be freed up. These two strands signal a change of focus away from heroic leaders, who normally reside in the upper echelons of organizations, and towards a focus on teams as repositories of leadership.

The third expression of the dispersed leadership tradition can be seen in the suggestion that there should be much greater attention paid to leadership processes and skills, which may or may not reside in formally designated leaders. There is much written about leadership skills. Even special editions are devoted to the topic. The problem is that much of it relates to the formally designated leader – in other words, the manager. Hosking (1988; 1991) conceptualized leadership in terms of an 'organizing' activity and spells out some of the distinctive features of leadership in terms of such a perspective. For example, she identified 'networking' as a particularly notable organizing skill among leaders, in which the cultivation and exercise of wider social influence is a key ingredient. But such a skill is not the exclusive preserve of formally appointed leaders. Indeed, it is the activity of networking and its effects that are critical to understanding the distinctiveness of leadership. The grounded theory method provides insights into the social processes of leadership. Parts of those social processes are activities or skills that leaders undertake. However, the lie of the land is still shrouded in fog, and the nature of the dispersal of leadership is still unclear.

In a similar vein to Hosking, Knights and Willmott (1992) advocated greater attention to what they called the 'practices' of leadership. This emphasis means looking at how leadership is constituted in organizations, so that in their study of a series of verbal exchanges at a meeting in a British financial services company, they show how the chief executive's definition of the situation is made to predominate. Unfortunately the distinctiveness of this research, and Hosking's (1991) investigation of Australian chief executives and of much leadership research coming out of North America, is marred somewhat by a focus on designated leaders. As a result, it is difficult to disentangle leadership as skill or activity from leadership as position. However, the potential implication of these ideas is to project an image of leadership as much more diffuse and dispersed within organizations than would be evident from the tendency for leadership to be viewed as the preserve of very few formally-designated leaders. The point here is that demonstrating leadership makes you a leader; and not the other way round. Wherein you are nominated as a leader, and then expected to shoulder the burden of demonstrating most of the leadership. What usually happens in organizational settings, however, is that one is appointed as a 'manager' and is then expected to shoulder the burdens of leadership. Clearly therefore, the notion of the distribution of leadership is not a part of the traditional organizational experience of managerial appointment.

A fourth expression of distributed leadership is Gordon's (2002) distinction between dispersed and traditional leadership discourse. By using observation and discourse analysis within an organizational setting, Gordon asserts that the deep power structures of organizations serve to maintain traditional notions of differentiation between leader and follower, with low levels of sharing of power and information. This high differentiation adversely affects the behaviour of team members. Further, Gordon asserts that organizations frequently have surface-level, or espoused empowerment, but serve to maintain domination at the deep structure levels. The surface-level empowerment includes the discourse of empowerment, the flattening of hierarchy and the act of delegation. However, the deep power structures are represented by such things as seating arrangements, intimidating language, deference, implied threat, offensive humour, and the allocation of rewards – among many others. By so doing, the deep power structures serve to reinforce pre-existing leadership relativities, in spite of the rhetoric and discourse of the distribution of power that those in senior positions would have followers believe.

By contrast, Collins (2001b) asserts that level 5 leadership, a combination of humility and fierce resolve, will enhance leader credibility and achieve genuine empowerment and the motivation of followers to achieve optimum performance. Level 5 leadership is pitched at the individual level of analysis. However, it seems to reflect a more genuine attempt at distributing leadership and at overcoming the effect of deep power structures, whether implicitly or explicitly. Clearly, more research is needed into the concept of level 5 leadership, and into the impact of deep power structures upon the distribution of leadership.

A fifth expression of distributed leadership, according to Parry and Bryman (2006), is leadership within the context of e-commerce (Brown and Gioia, 2002) or an advanced information technology environment (Avolio et al., 2001). The technology associated with e-commerce and with advanced technology systems, also called Group Support Systems (GSS; Sosik et al., 1997) provides particular challenges for leadership. Ken first met John Sosik at Binghamton, New York in 1993 when Ken went there to be inspired by Bass and Avolio, and John was a PhD student there. John was researching e-leadership and Group Support Systems, as that area of research was taking off. As we speak, it is still a priority and John Sosik is still one of the key names in the area.

On the one hand, senior managers are able to get information to large groups of followers quickly and in large volume. On the other hand, group members can access large amounts of information independently of their leaders. In effect, managers lose much control over information flow and the power that goes with it. Avolio et al. (2001) conclude that in some settings, people can observe and model from others how they should interact. By doing this, technology becomes part of the social transformation in the organization, and in turn, part of the leadership process. In other settings, other leaders may view the technology as a cost-effective way of controlling employee behaviour through constant monitoring of deviations from standards. This latter style of leadership is likely to generate a very different social system from the former. This latter style reads much like Gordon's issue with deep power structures that reinforce the existing allocations of power and influence.

Brown and Gioia (2002) found that the e-commerce environment was characterized by speed, ambiguity and complexity. They agree with Avolio et al. (2001) that not only is leadership influenced by this context, but also integrated with and even defined by it. To Brown and Gioia, leadership is not solely a set of characteristics possessed by an individual but an emergent property of a social system, in which 'leaders' and 'followers' share in the process of enacting leadership. The notion here is very clear: that effective leadership depends upon multiple leaders for decision-making and action-taking. With the interest of people like Bruce Avolio, John Sosik, Brown, Gioia and others, the future of this research is assured. Once again, the key to success lies in distributing leadership across the population and not concentrating it within the workloads of a few.

Much more research is needed into how the process of leadership is operationalized in the e-commerce environment. One reason for this need is that the speed and depth of change in this area of life continues unabated. Every time you need a software upgrade or a new anti-virus definition for your computer, you know that the real leaders are the people with the control over the technology. You get the point. The other reason is that we have only touched the surface of our knowledge about how leadership can or should operate in this brave new world. Processual research is needed. Questionnaire-based research is unlikely to achieve the level of insight and depth of understanding that is required. In these five sets of writings, we can see an alternative perspective that emphasizes the importance of recognizing the need for leadership to be viewed as a widely dispersed activity which is not necessarily lodged in formally designated leaders.

leaderless work groups

In a similar vein, there exist literatures on self-managed work teams, self-directed work teams, and leaderless work groups. A milder version of this concept is that of 'semi-autonomous work groups'. In these situations, much of the responsibility and authority usually invested in a manager's position, is turned over to the team members.

Much of the research work on these self-managing teams was done in manufacturing industry or process work. Certainly, it was undertaken within an organizational or business environment. Team members usually have similar backgrounds, namely of trade or technical experience. They usually take turns performing the various tasks and thus generate flexibility and a degree of job enrichment. The tasks performed by self-managing teams are usually of the day-to-day administrative nature, and include setting work schedules, dealing directly with external customers, setting performance targets and conducting training (Gordon, 1992). Many of the larger-scale or 'visionary' aspects of leadership are not part of their scope of activities. Therefore, much of the higher-level or 'macro' aspects of leadership still have to be undertaken by the external leadership role, specifically the senior manager. Consequently, we could conclude that it is difficult to do away with a person in the primary leadership role. In other words, an organization or work unit must always have someone 'in charge', even in a so-called leaderless work group.

In a sense, we are really just discussing one aspect of organizational structure rather than a leadership issue in organizations. Notions of authority, accountability, span of control, unity of command and suchlike still have to be taken into account when organizing any work group. However, it is the issue of what is 'going on' between people that really determines the nature of the leadership that is represented in that group of people.

Having said that, great improvements have been reported in self-managed work teams. The research has mainly been in the form of various types of case studies. Examples include the work of Banker et al. (1996), Cohen and Ledford (1994), Cordery et al. (1991), and Pearson (1992). Research into leaderless work groups and self-managed work teams has diminished in recent years. Methodologically, there is the potential problem that most research is self-report. The empirical evidence varies greatly and the self-report nature of many write-ups throws doubt on the extent to which leadership really has been dispersed within the work groups. To be sure, self-managed work teams and leaderless work groups may well be an effective way to achieve manufacturing output. However, perhaps the most telling insight comes from Barker (1993).

Barker researched self-managing teams. His fascinating work is genuine ethnography, and with no inherent bias toward the organization. It is no longer new research but it is class work, and class work will always live on. He provided an ethnographic account of how an organization's control system evolved in response to a managerial change form hierarchical, bureaucratic control to 'concertive' control in the from of self-managing teams. Members developed a system of value-based normative rules that controlled their actions more powerfully and completely than the former system. Concertive control evolved from the value consensus of the company's team workers to a system of normative rules that became increasingly rationalized and normalized. In spite of the newly de-layered and empowered environment, people began to develop their own norms, rules and expectations of each other. They also developed their own hierarchy and formal leadership roles. These emergent structures were even more powerful than before because they were developed by the workers themselves and not imposed from above. In effect, they could not be escaped. Contrary to the beliefs of some advocates of such systems, concertive control did not free these workers from bureaucratic control. Instead, concertive control appeared to draw the 'iron cage' of bureaucratic control even tighter to constrain organizational members even more powerfully.

To the literature on self-managing teams, Barker has added the concept of concertive control. Perhaps one leadership outcome of the creation of self-managed teams is to create more powerful normative control over co-workers. If that is what is intended as a leadership outcome, then self-managed teams are successful. However, such an outcome flies in the face of much of the contemporary literature on the processual nature of leadership. After all, leadership is meant to empower workers and create innovation rather than impose more powerful control mechanisms. Perhaps self-managing teams have the opposite effect from what is normally expected by contemporary notions of 'leadership'. Perhaps self-managing teams actually inhibit innovation and empowerment. Certainly, they appear to reduce individual discretion through the impact of concertive control. If so, a conclusion might be that people might need *some degree* of self-leadership (or self-management), but *in addition* they might continue to need the more traditional formal leadership role to achieve the expression of the 'visionary' and macro aspects of leadership.

Ironically, since the work of Barker was published, we have seen a reduction in the volume of new literature on self-managed teams. This is not to say that this is the end of the story ... far from it. We do need to work out what we really are trying to research in this field. There is the opportunity for more ethnography to unveil how and why these phenomena operate. Just as concertive control emerged, so might other very illuminating constructs also emerge.

Our sense is that the leaderless work group is really just an oxymoron. Humans still need direction, control, rules, hierarchy, predictability, routine and so on. Any work unit must have a person in the primary leadership role. In other words, there must be an appointed manager. The issue at stake is the extent to which leader*ship* can be distributed among the various people who constitute that group. If that leadership is distributed effectively, one starts to move from a group to a team. This brings us on to the matter of team leadership.

team leadership

Theoretical and conceptual discussion about team leadership abounds, and much of it overlaps with discussion about 'shared' leadership (see, for example, Pearce and Sims, 2000). The notion of team leadership measures leadership as a group-level construct, and looks at leadership 'by' the team rather than 'of' the team or 'in' the team. However, research into team or shared leadership is still scarce. One exception is Avolio et al. (2003) on the validation of the Team Multifactor Leadership Questionnaire (TMLQ). Another is Mayo et al.'s (2003) social network approach. Although this latter work is about the process of social network analysis and the value of it as a research tool, rather than an actual report on a completed research project, the possibilities are opened up for researchers to pick up this ball and run with it. Social network analysis is useful for understanding the dynamics of shared leadership in work teams for three reasons. First, shared leadership is a relational construct and would benefit from a relational approach such as social network analysis. Second, the unit of analysis is the relation and not the leader or follower. Third, the essence of leadership is influence, and social network analysis examines the nature of influence networks.

Shamir and Lapidot (2003) adopted the perspective of shared leadership as a reciprocal influence process among multiple parties in a systems context. They examined the narrative surrounding certain critical incidents in a military environment, to test for the form and effect of those reciprocal influence processes. Data that were gathered included questionnaire responses, group interviews and individual interviews. They provided a fascinating insight into the notions of collective power, leader (in this case 'commander') vulnerability, shared values and shared identity. Narrative analysis provides huge scope for research into leadership. Boje's (2001) text is the best insight into these methods. He proposes a range of methodologies by which narrative analysis can be undertaken.

One problem with research into team leadership is that people have an intrinsic fear of the notion of leadership by a team, rather than leadership by an individual or individuals. For example, this fear can be represented by potential research questions like 'How does a board of directors demonstrate leadership?' When gripped with this fear, the natural reaction is to think that the board is a collection of people and it is those individuals who demonstrate leadership. Therefore, team leadership is little more than multiple individual leaderships represented concurrently. After all, people come and go from the board, so the 'board' is changed every time there is a change in membership. On the other hand the team, namely the board, is still providing leadership even though the membership of the team changes. It is a little like a winning sporting team that leads the competition. For various reasons, including injury and loss of form, individuals are replaced from time to time, but the team still leads the competition over time. The team, in effect, demonstrates leadership.

Therefore, the challenge for the research mindset is to distinguish the individuals on the board from the collective entity itself. The research question is about how the collective entity demonstrates leadership, and NOT how the individuals behave. We have used the 'board' as one example. Other examples of leadership teams might include sporting teams, as we have said, or political parties, societal groupings, fashion designers and even companies demonstrating market leadership. Brad Jackson's (2001) work on management fads and fashions, utilizing dramatistic inquiry and fantasy theme analysis, is one such example. He researched management gurus, but if the subject of the inquiry is the fad or fashion, and not the person, then the new direction of the research becomes a very exciting insight into team leadership. This is a very fertile direction for leadership research in the near future.

The conclusion to be drawn thus far is that everyone can display leadership. Such an outcome reduces the role of formal leaders. Groups cannot do without a formal leader, but team leadership reduces the pressure on the formal leader to produce all the leadership. However, before we get too carried away with models of distributional leadership, Grint (2005) offers us some grounds for caution. He notes that some forms of distributive leadership may be attractive to people who are inhibited by idiosyncratic leaders or who are being suffocated by stultifying bureaucracies. Even so, simply wishing away leadership, 'the big pink elephant' as he colourfully characterizes it, may result in some grossly ineffective and inefficient organizations that can become susceptible to takeover by authoritarian leaders.

Moreover, distributed leadership can also generate the means by which liberal democratic societies can be destabilized by small and unrepresentative groups or even individuals. By way of graphic example, Grint brings us bang smack up to date with a sobering and trenchant account of the rise and persistence of the hydra-like terrorist group, al-Qaida. Grint concludes that distributed leadership presents us with a serious paradox: 'it provides something of a blueprint for making us face the terror of the pink elephant, for *inhibiting* authoritarian leaders, but it also provides terrorists with a blueprint for *cohabiting* with what seems to be leaderless authoritarianism' (2005: 145).

conclusion

In this chapter we have looked at more critically-oriented perspectives of leadership. They all share a common concern with the concentration of power in the hands of a few nominal leaders as well as a general dissatisfaction with the hierarchical, top-down models of leadership that have dominated conventional leadership thinking since time immemorial. These leadership thinkers attempt to develop alternative either more 'leaderful' or 'leaderless' leadership models which enable followers to take on leadership responsibilities either at the top of the organization, through co- or shared leadership models or throughout the organization through the creation of dispersed leadership models. While there is plenty of support for these post-heroic or anti-heroic normative modes of leadership, there is still – as yet – a paucity of empirical models of organizations that have successfully created and sustained distributed models of leadership over the longer term.

This is not to denigrate in any way these well-meaning theorizing efforts, but it does give one pause for thought as to the viability and indeed desirability of these alternative models. We remain continually impressed by the influence that leaders at the top of an organization can have, either for good or bad. We tend both to overestimate and to underestimate the influence that these leaders hold over their followers. After all, it is the followers who get the work done and ultimately decide whether or not an organization will either succeed or fail. That being said, the leaders continue to play an important role in influencing followers' beliefs about whether or not a goal is worth pursuing and whether or not they have the ability to achieve that goal successfully. Our stance, therefore, is not to turn our backs on hierarchical forms of leadership simply because we do not trust or like hierarchy. We remain more concerned with the ends of leadership rather than its means. This is why we continue to find ways to invigorate the existing leader-centric models of leadership and to refine and bolster follower-centric models of leadership by means of maintaining a healthy democratic counterbalance.

6

Leadership with a Higher Purpose

'The ethics of leadership rests upon three pillars: (1) the moral character of the leader; (2) the ethical legitimacy of the values embedded in the leader's vision, articulation, and program which followers either embrace or reject; and (3) the morality of the processes of social ethical choice and action that leaders and followers engage in and collectively pursue'.

Bass and Steidlmeier, 1999: 182

introduction

The ways in which we study leadership must involve much more than just how one person gets other people to follow their lead. If we restrict our implicit theory of leadership to mere following, then *everything* becomes leadership. Of course, if everything is leadership then nothing is leadership. This is far too trite an approach to what we all speculate is a much more complex topic. Let us provide an example that is often cited in popular press writings and tutorial-room discussions about leadership. That example is the leadership of Adolf Hitler. Many people cite Adolf Hitler as a leader. We have always had difficulty with this claim when discussing Hitler in executive development programmes. To those people who believe that Adolf Hitler was a leader Ken asks for the aspects of his leadership that they will adopt for themselves. 'What parts of Hitler's leadership will become part of your leadership?' Would they adopt the dramatic histrionics of the mass rally? Would they copy the brutal bullying of those who disagree? Would they exploit a desperate and hungry population and lead them ultimately into an even more catastrophic destiny? Would they adopt the lies and hubris, and the resultant vilification of a 'common enemy'? Does the end really justify the means? You probably get the point. People start to question whether Hitler was a leader or just a tyrant. Hitler certainly got people to follow him, but there must be more to leadership than just getting people to follow. Hitler is hardly a role model for leadership training courses today. I am aware of no such courses on 'How to be an Adolf Hitler for your organization'. If Adolf Hitler was a leader, and if Adolf Hitler demonstrated leadership, then 'anything goes'. We really must look past charisma and into the motives of the leader. We must look past leader behaviours and into the heart of the leader. We really need to have an insight into leadership for a higher purpose. This process has begun, but it has a long way to go.

authentic leadership

As an opening example, Bass and Steidlmeier (1999) have acknowledged the differences between authentic and what they call pseudo-transformational leadership. They argue that authentic transformational leadership is more than just behaving in a transformational way. This is not a reason to stop studying transformational leadership; this is just a reason to study it further and with greater epistemological diversity. They argue that authentic (transformational) leadership is grounded on moral and virtuous foundations. Whereas an authentic transformational leader will focus on universal values, the pseudo-transformational leader might highlight 'our' values against 'their' values and generate conflict. Whereas an authentic transformational leader will sound the alarm when real threats arise, the pseudo-transformational leader might manufacture crises where none exist. Whereas an authentic transformational leader will develop followers into leaders, the pseudo-transformational leader might develop submissive disciples. Both leaders will achieve these very different outcomes by *behaving* in essentially the same way.

Under the heading of individualized consideration, true transformational leaders are concerned about developing their followers into leaders, helping those followers to become more competent, and to provide for successful succession to a leadership role. The inauthentic leader is concerned about maintaining the dependence of followers and maintaining something akin to a parent-child relationship. Under the heading of intellectual stimulation, true transformational leaders are concerned about persuading others of the merits of certain issues. They bring about changes in followers' values by the merit and relevancy of the leader's ideas for the ultimate benefit of the followers. The inauthentic pseudo-transformational leader will set and control an agenda in order to manipulate the values of importance to followers for the benefit of the leader and to the detriment of followers.

Under the heading of inspirational and visionary leadership, the inspirational appeals of authentic transformational leaders focus on the best in people – on harmony, charity and good work. The inspirational appeals of the pseudo-transformational leader will focus on the worst in people – on plots, conspiracies and insecurities. These people mislead, deceive and prevaricate; they offer empowerment but continue to seek control. In terms of the charismatic aspects of the idealized leader, the true transformational leader is confident and sets high standards for emulation. On the other hand, the pseudo-transformational leader will seek power and position, even at the expense of their followers' achievements. This person will argue that they are working for the good of the organization but work for their own benefit, even if it is to the detriment of the organization. This person is inconsistent and unreliable.

You can perhaps see that we are delving into the moral authenticity of the leader. We contend that the moral authenticity of the leader explains the authenticity of that person's leader*ship*. As Gardner et al. have observed from their extensive research into authentic leadership 'we are struck by the uplifting effects of lower profile but genuine leaders who lead by example in fostering healthy ethical climates characterised by transparency, trust, integrity, and high moral standards. We call such leaders authentic leaders who are not only true to themselves, but lead others by helping them to likewise achieve authenticity' (2005: 344).

Our conclusion is that there is a great need to study the authenticity of leadership much further. Certainly, we need also to study 'inauthentic' leadership, but we need to discriminate between the two. Indeed, the notion of polarity, or the study of these polar opposites, is hugely illuminating for a researcher. Hence, we have further motivation to move our study of leadership past the behaviours and goals of people in leadership roles. We must move to an appreciation of the motives and values of these people. Indeed, we even need to move toward an examination of their unconscious or tacit motivations for enacting leadership in the way that they do. Studies such as this might have to move past the objective or tangible data that we normally use for our case studies drawn from questionnaires, interviews and observations.

Research such as in the direction we are now heading might require a critical realist perspective, wherein the deeper underlying causal influences that shape leadership are investigated. For example, people might be learning to lead in the course of their careers, and not even know how they are learning to lead. Therefore, we cannot study this leadership phenomenon by interviewing or surveying these people, because they don't really know what they are talking about. How can they talk about how they learn leadership when they don't even know that they are learning it? The work of Steve Kempster (2006) provides a useful starting point for investigations into research such as this. An extension of this problem is that people might be leading in a certain way and not even be aware of the underlying moral structure that determines their actions. Therefore, we cannot study this aspect of leadership by interviewing or surveying these people, because they are not even consciously aware of their underlying moral structure and values. Such research would move past the grounded theory and case study methods to elaborate Bhaskar's (1989) notion of retroductive argument in order to uncover the underlying or 'deep' causal influences on people in leadership positions.

As a general rule, 'critical management studies' resides in the UK, and the objective epistemologies reside more popularly in North America than elsewhere. Having said that, the North American Academy of Management has interest groups in 'Critical Management Studies' and in 'Management Spirituality and Religion'. Admittedly, they are interest groups and not the more formal divisions of the Academy, but it goes to show that you cannot generalize in these matters. As always, Europe and Australasia draw upon all empirical orthodoxies roughly equally.

In effect, the recent interest in authentic leadership is reflective of a broader interest generally in the spirituality of leadership.

the spirituality of leadership

The movement away from the behaviours and styles of the transformational or charismatic leader, indeed the move away from behavioural styles of leadership generally, has also led to an interest in the spirituality of leadership. Conversations about the dark side of charisma, narcissism and pseudo-transformational leadership have led inevitably to theoretical discussion about the 'right' and 'wrong' of leadership, rather than just the utilitarian effectiveness of leadership. After all, Bass's original (1985) notion of transformational leadership included the role of enabling followers to transcend their interests above the day-to-day transactional concerns and to take inspiration from emotional appeals to a higher spiritual level of interest. The notion is not new, but interest in it is escalating as the twenty-first century unfolds.

While much of the discussion at the end of the twentieth century had a theological side to it, authors such as Hicks (2002) are at pains to differentiate leadership from religious or theological matters. As Hicks notes, there are a number of characteristics of leadership that resonate in the mainstream literature, which have a spiritual tone to them. These characteristics include self-actualization and self-awareness, authenticity, the management of meaning, emotion and passion, intrinsic motivation, wisdom, discernment, courage, transcendence, and interconnectedness – as well as the more traditional leadership subjects of morality, integrity, values, honesty and justice. Any person who is interested in studying leadership should be aware of these concepts, and be prepared to integrate them into the study in some way. However, it is unwise simply to conclude that leadership is about living a good life and being a good Christian or Muslim or Hindu, or whatever. Rather, to avoid throwing 50 years of leadership research out with the bath water, any theory of spiritual leadership should demonstrate its utility through its ability to impact favourably upon organizational performance (Sass, 2000), or certainly an ability to achieve some form of common utility, as well as its ability to discern right from wrong and morally to uplift leader and follower alike.

Fry's (2003) theory of spiritual leadership posits that leader values, attitudes and behaviours, which essentially are covered comprehensively within the extant leadership literature, will generate outcomes via the intrinsic motivation of followers. Further, it posits that intrinsic motivation is a factor of followers' needs for spiritual survival. Those needs are met through being understood and appreciated, and by a feeling that life has meaning for them and that they can make a difference. In one sense, it could be argued that followers' needs for spiritual survival are merely a reiteration of Shamir's self-concept theory (1993) of motivation blended with Pye's (2005) sense-making and Smircich's management of meaning theory (1993). On the other hand, more realistically, Fry's theory is a comprehensive examination of how these more recent leadership concepts come to have their ultimate impact upon outcomes such as organizational performance. The spiritual leadership literature is also an effective and persuasive way to integrate and make sense of concepts as disparate as altruistic love, honesty and integrity on the one hand and narcissism and pseudo-transformational leadership on the other.

In a sense, the literature on spirituality is about the spirituality of leadership rather than a new theory of spiritual leadership. The latter reads like a new type of leadership, which the literature is not suggesting. Instead, the spirituality literature attempts to make better sense of the extant leadership literature. It is a fascinating new and fruitful area of leadership research, and one well worth pursuing. Interestingly, a Google search in early 2007 came up with 493 hits for 'spirituality quotient'. As you would expect, this term relates to a questionnaire that gives a score for one's SQ, or spirituality quotient. Thankfully, the SQ has not entered the academic arena to any large degree, and we hope that it remains within the popular press and consulting arena. However, the point is well made that the spirituality of leadership is here to stay. We have no doubt that there will ultimately be a questionnaire to measure spirituality, but we earnestly hope that the study of the spirituality of leadership will be much more broad-based and explanatory than a questionnaire.

post-charismatic and post-transformational leadership

The implication thus far is that there is much more to transformational and charismatic leadership than just behaviours and outcomes. This realization has led to the emergence of what is being called post-charismatic and post-transformational leadership, for want of a better term. Parry and Bryman (2006) have provided an examination of this emerging label for the study of leadership. Storey (2004) suggested that transformational and charismatic leadership were very much constructs of the late twentieth century. The technology of the time and the prevailing management orthodoxies were very much those of the heroic or capable individual leader being able to transform corporations and transform the perceptions and motivations of people within those corporations. And yes, it was mainly 'corporations' that dominated the discourse, and not 'organizations' or 'society'. The increasingly distributed nature of leadership, combined with concerns about narcissistic and pseudo-transformational leaders and the shadow or 'dark' side of charisma, has led to a more recent conceptualization of leadership for organizations.

Fullan (2001) bases this new and implicit model of 'post-charismatic' or 'post-transformational' leadership around embedded learning, truly distributed leadership in teams, and learning from experience and failure. Leadership practice is more consciously made public and open to challenge and testing. Some major failures of corporate leadership at the turn of the century have provided fertile ground for the uptake of these ideas. Names like Enron have become archetypes for the problematic side of leadership that seems to dominate scholarship these days. The upside of case studies such as these is that they have heightened the need for alternate conceptualizations of leadership and for appropriate ways to study them.

For example, by examining the life and achievements of Benjamin Franklin, Mumford and Van Doorn (2001) proposed a theory of pragmatic leadership which would help to meet the shortfalls of the transformational, transactional and charismatic approaches. Transformational and charismatic leadership rely overly upon communication of values and ideals, while transactional leadership relies overly upon control and the exercise of power. Mumford and Van Doorn argued that something other than transformational and transactional leadership explained exceptional leadership. They engaged in a historiographic case study of Benjamin Franklin. Not only is the theory and conceptualization of the research problem post-transformational, but the research methodology certainly is as well. They chose a case study upon which there is considerable data. Not only that, but the figure in question is sufficiently historical that subjective attributions about the moral authenticity of his leadership – normally a potential weakness in research – have probably lapsed.

Mumford and Van Doorn argued that pragmatic leaders exercise influence by identifying and communicating solutions to significant social problems, meeting the practical needs of followers, working through elites in solution generation, creating structures to support solution implementation, and demonstrating the feasibility of these solutions. These tactics might not make much sense at first glance here, but the article is a rollicking good read and well worth the effort involved in looking it up. Franklin utilized these tactics to achieve, among other things, the establishment of subscription libraries, the municipal police department, volunteer fire department, road paving and lighting, and the University of Pennsylvania. To some cynical people, these leadership tactics might sound like little more than (organizational) politics. Certainly, the political process of leadership – that of working through elites and communicating solutions to a wider fraternity of people – is necessary. We would contend further that though it is necessary, it is not sufficient. After all, organizational politics for its own sake is non-authentic and self-serving leadership. Abraham Zaleznik was writing about organizational politics in 1970. In recent years, Jeffrey Pfeffer and Edgar Schein have led the scholarship about the politics of the organization. It is not a new concept within the huge extant literature on leadership.

Other cynical people might contend that Franklin's strategy is what we would now call the triple bottom line or social responsibility. These are populist terms, but still are worthy of study. Still other cynical people might contend that Franklin did little more than create an early form of 'frequent flyer points', by demonstrating to people the personal financial benefit that they could accrue by coming on board with his visions.

The frequent flyer points analogy might be unfair or it might be accurate, but either way, there is a leadership message inherent within the Benjamin Franklin case study. The message is that this 'pragmatic' aspect of leadership is more than just an engaging in a transaction. It is about showing a population the tangible benefits that accrue by being a part of major societal change and innovation. The point we make is that these issues are not yet contained within contemporary approaches to the research of leadership.

the art of leadership

Given the increased expectations placed upon leaders to foster creativity and innovation within and beyond their organizations, an increasing number of leadership commentators have argued that we should be looking not just to the sciences but also to the arts to help us make sense of and develop leadership. Most persuasively, in his book *The Arts of Leadership*, Keith Grint (2001) has observed, 'if we abandon the infinite quest for scientific certainty and seek out the philosophical, fine, martial, and performing arts, we might go some way to resolving the most perennial of human questions: what is leadership?'. Effective leaders, he argues, need to develop and learn from an ensemble of arts.

From the philosophical arts, leaders can learn to create a compelling sense of identity for their organization (i.e. who are we?); from the fine arts they can learn to forge a powerful strategic vision for the organizations they lead (i.e. where are we going?); from the martial arts they can learn to develop smart organizational tactics (i.e. how will we achieve this?); and from the performing arts, they can learn to persuasively communicate to their followers the organization's identity, its strategic vision and its tactics.

Rosener (1997) and Calás and Smircich (1997) looked at leadership through the lens of gender stereotyping and concluded that mainstream leadership literature has traditionally been couched in masculine terms and that leadership can be interpreted as seduction. This is but one metaphor for leadership. There are many more. Three that we like are parenting, schooling and captaincy. We are doing more than just engaging in the art of word games; these metaphors help us make sense of the leadership challenge that managers face. These metaphors are supported not just by fifty years of research, but also by the implicit ideas that so many clients and students have brought to us in executive development and teaching courses we have conducted.

Michael Michalko (2001) has written that metaphors dominate the discourse of geniuses. The thought and talk of people with very high IQs are dominated by metaphors and analogies. We should remember that the craft of the wordsmith is central to the effectiveness of managers in their leadership role. Keith Grint would probably say that the craft of the wordsmith is central to enacting the performing art of leadership. We will spend a little time examining the above three metaphors, because the further investigation of metaphors is an important ongoing direction for the study of leadership.

leadership as parenting

Those of us who are parents realize that we are charged with a grave responsibility. A responsibility … I hear you say … a grave responsibility? Is there another kind? Parenting is the gravest of responsibilities. We develop our children from a state of complete dependency, through ever-increasing levels of independence and autonomy, until ultimately they are fully independent self-reliant adults. We are role models for them. We must provide the information and resources they need to be able to grow and develop. We must develop and train (in other words, educate) them. We must provide the knowledge they need to make sense of the otherwise confusing state of affairs that constitutes growing up. We must provide a healthy and safe environment for them. We must protect them from violence and harassment. They are a reflection upon us as parents.

Exactly the same responsibility confronts the challenge of leadership in our society more broadly. OK – take away the nappies and baby stuff, but the role of leadership is the same thing as parenting. Let's take organizational leadership as an example. As leaders we develop followers from dependency to autonomy – let's call that empowerment, for want of a less 'faddish' term. We are role models for our employees. We have a legal responsibility to provide the information and resources to enable people to do their jobs. We also have a legal responsibility to provide a healthy and safe environment for employees. We must provide developmental opportunities and knowledge. The culture of the workplace is an eye into the leadership of that workplace. Yes, leadership is parenting.

leadership as schooling

Schooling develops children through adolescence into adulthood, just as leadership develops followers from dependence to autonomy. Schooling involves conformity and control as well as knowledge and independence. So too does managerial leadership in organizations. Schooling involves teaching, training, mentoring, developing. So too does leadership. Schooling has hierarchy and structure. So too does leadership. Schooling involves rewards as well as punishments. So too does leadership. Yes, leadership is like schooling.

leadership as captaincy

We use the dual metaphor of captaincy of a sporting team and captaincy as a military rank. The captain of a sporting team is a role model on and off the field, as is the leader. The captain of the sporting team ensures teamwork on the sports field, as does the leader. The captain of the sporting team enacts the game plan, as does the leader. The military captain provides for the welfare and morale of the troops, as does the leader. The military captain fights the good fight, as does the leader. The military captain puts her (or his) welfare before that of the troops, as does the leader. Yes, leadership is also captaincy.

We can see a common thread through the above metaphors. The metaphors help us make sense of the leadership challenge that we all face. Therefore, there is a sense-making thread. Let us now take you through sense-making as the essence of leadership.

sense-making and the art of leadership

A number of scholars have attempted to distil the essence of leadership – to integrate all those messages and mottos and mantras down into one overarching message. As we have already said, Smircich and Morgan said it was the management of meaning. Bass and Avolio said it was transforming the hearts and minds of followers. In Ken's PhD research some years ago, he found that the essence of leadership was in enhancing the adaptability of people to the turbulence and uncertainty of change. Karl Weick and Annie Pye said the essence of leadership was sense-making. All these people are saying much the same thing, but this final one resonates the most with me.

Sense-making is when people understand the vision and are not just following a plan; it comes from face-to-face personal contact not from distant impersonal contact; it comes from delegation not control. Sense-making enables people to act and not just react; it enables them to take risks and not just avoid risk; it enables people to initiate change and not just accommodate it. Yes, sense-making is the essence of leadership.

This sense-making can be achieved through *science*. The science of sense-making about leadership is very important to note because it has formed the basis of the vast majority of leadership research for many years. The science of sense-making about leadership has come from experimental research, from quantitative content analysis, from questionnaire-survey research. Strongly influenced by psychology and economics, the science of sense-making has given us structures and equations and models and structural equation modelling. Science has given us a huge amount of sense-making. But it goes only so far. Art complements science to help our sense-making.

Sense-making can be achieved through verbal techniques such as metaphor and analogy. You have already read how the use of metaphors helps us to make sense of the nature of leadership. Similarly, metaphors help leaders to convey meaning to followers. The Chief Executive might call himself the 'Chief Enthusiasm Officer', as does a colleague in Brisbane who is CEO of one of the biggest retail food companies in the country. The marketing plan could be a 'sure bet' or it could be 'Russian roulette'. We use them all the time. We could and should use them more to rev-up the usefulness of most 'management-speak'.

Sense-making can also be achieved through the use of humour. Humour is another art form. Humour brings out all the paradoxes, ambiguities and ironies associated with mixed messages, and in so doing resolves them in the hearts and minds of followers. Refreshingly, research by people like Avolio et al. (1999b) supports this point. Humour is a sense-making activity. The use of humour helps make leadership more effective.

Sense-making can be achieved through another art form, the art of poetry. For example, Japanese haiku poetry can convey extraordinarily complex messages in one 17-syllable 3-line poem. Try it out for yourself – 5-syllables, 7-syllables, 5-syllables – three lines of poetry.

Rick Brenner uses Haiku to teach project management. This one highlights the problems associated with expedient solutions:

> Our project was late
> So we added more people
> The problem got worse

This one came from work Ken did with a government agency, and reflects the cynicism and scorn so often triggered by organizational change:

> We want leadership
> Must have self-managed work teams
> Try again next year

You can combine poetry with humour. This example from the Internet humorously highlights the simple frustrations associated with computer glitches:

> Your file was so big.
> It might be very useful.
> But now it is gone.

They are powerful sense-making. They are leadership. OK, we are not so conceited or superficial as to suggest that the leadership challenges that face senior managers can be condensed into a three-line poem. We are saying that poetry is one way that the art of leadership can be understood and conveyed to an audience of followers. Sense-making art forms such as these could and should form the basis of future studies of leadership.

Sense-making can also be achieved through visual art. We know how a good frame will transform an otherwise lifeless painting into a virtual masterpiece. Hence, the notion of framing helps us to transform mere words into a persuasive argument. For example, we often hear people make comments like 'If we frame this challenge as a make-or-break moment, then our people will see the necessity of our strategy'. From visual art we get the notion of perspective. Articulating the long-term perspective helps employees see the relevance of decisions taken today. From visual art we also get the notion of neatness and tidiness. For example, marketing plans must have no 'loose ends'. Uncluttered work areas are not just a safety matter. They also provide a positive emotional impact on the hearts of workers, via a visual stimulus, such that they are more committed to the workplace.

Visual art gives us balance and symmetry. We must balance the books. Managers must find a balance between being consultative and being directive. Visual art provides aesthetics such as harmony, beauty, contrast and emphasis. Yes, sense-making is the essence of leadership and as leaders we can improve our sense-making through a better appreciation of visual art. Leadership is an art and not just a science. There is huge scope within a range of methods of discourse and narrative analysis to research the representation and impact of leadership as sense-making. These are ways that the craft of the wordsmith can help us to study and understand leadership, and to enact leadership. The main scholars in the discourse area are Cliff Oswick, Tom Keenoy and David Grant (Oswick et al., 2002). Along with Cynthia Hardy, they have produced many books and articles on discourse analysis with an emphasis on the utility of metaphors as data as well as being the subject of research. Additionally, David Boje's (2001) book is still the benchmark on narrative analysis in organizations.

But we need more. We need more than just having the topic and the interest and the research heritage. We also need people who can think like an artist or like a musician or like an actor *and* think like a leadership scholar. For many years leadership research has been driven by people who think like a psychologist or like a sociologist or like an economist or like a business manager. They have done great work and created great insights. But we need more. The era of the artistic and dramatic genre of leadership research is about to begin, we hope.

the art of leadership and bodily knowledge

The artistic or aesthetic approach to leadership involves more than merely using acting or art as metaphors for leadership. Ropo and Eriksson (1997) and Ropo et al. (2002) brought an aesthetic perspective to the study of leadership when they examined leadership as 'bodily' knowledge within the context of the performing arts industry. They asserted that a result of organizational leadership could be bodily knowledge, as distinct from cognitive knowledge or affective influence. Bodily knowledge is a type of tacit knowledge, derived from demonstration and learning-by-doing, and is conceptually similar to the 'sixth sense'. Just as the conductor of an orchestra might have a 'feel' for the music, the leader within an organization will have a 'feel' for what other employees are sensing and experiencing. Followers might 'feel their skin crawl' or 'feel it in their bones', or feel 'a presence' or have a 'gut-feel' about their leadership.

As far back as 1938 Chester Barnard (cited in Ottensmeyer 1996) cited terms pertinent to the executive process of management as being 'feeling', 'judgment', 'sense', 'proportion', 'balance' and 'appropriateness'. Perhaps we need to revisit classic works occasionally; and Barnard's is a classic work. We certainly don't want to reinvent wheels in a literature a big as that of leadership. Actually, we need to extend the work of Barnard, at long last, and investigate the artistic dimensions of leadership and the generation of bodily knowledge. Peter Cammock has captured the essence of leadership that future leaders will need to recognize and master when he states,

> Leadership is a dance, in which leaders and followers jointly respond to the rhythm and call for a particular social context, within which leaders draw from deep wells of collective experience and energy, to engage followers around transforming visions of change and led them in the collective creation of compelling futures. (Cammock, 2002)

The appreciation of the art of leadership is not new. In researching R&D knowledge-intensive work, Alvesson and Sveningsson (2003) found an inherent ambiguity of senior management in that this work was found to be characterized by incoherence, contradiction, confusion and fragmentation instead of the coherence, pattern and predictability which many years of leadership literature have led us to expect will result from visions, values and strategies. This ambiguity was reflected in the discourse which emerged from the leaders of the organization. The ideals that are reflected in the leadership discourse were found to be contradicted by the discourse of 'micro-management' that leaders must engage in. This ambiguous muddle presents an 'ugly' or 'unaesthetic' or 'grotesque' and, therefore, unappealing side to organizational leadership.

leadership as drama

As scholars, we are continuing to see a need to move from the investigation of the cause–effect challenge of leadership as science, and move on to the cause–affect sense-making of leadership as art. In particular, we are looking now at leadership as drama.

Just like actors in movies … as a leader, you play a part (it might be the CEO part); you have a role to play (it might be good guy or it might be bad guy or it might be change agent); you have a script (it might be the address to the Board or the off-the-cuff chat to employees); you have a costume (it might be the business suit, but it will vary depending on the screenplay); you have an audience (employees or media, or board members or other managers); you have a plot (it might be high drama or it might be a farce or it might be black comedy); you have a setting (it might be the committee meeting or the corridor); you have an emotional impact on the audience (it might be arousal or pride or surprise or disappointment or apprehension) … and finally, you have the sense-making that you want the audience to take away. Hopefully it will be a profitable production. This is leadership.

When we look at the female lead character in the movie *The Aviator*, do we say, 'wow, that is Cate Blanchett' or do we say, 'wow, that is Katherine Hepburn'. Probably, most of us would say, 'that is Cate Blanchett'. But, being the great actor that she is, we would ultimately be engrossed in watching Katherine Hepburn unfold before us as the movie progresses. Over time, we might almost be persuaded that we are actually watching Katherine Hepburn. It is still Cate Blanchett, but she is acting out a part very convincingly.

Let us make this point very clearly. Cate Blanchett was trying to be Katherine Hepburn. She was trying to be someone else. People in leadership roles are not actually actors. They are not trying to be someone else. They are *not* trying to be Winston Churchill, Martin Luther King, Margaret Thatcher, Gandhi, Adolf Hitler, or indeed Katherine Hepburn or anyone else. People in leadership roles should try to be their authentic selves to be successful. If potential followers think they are trying to impersonate someone else, they will lose credibility and, therefore, their following.

Instead, we are all acting out our own role and if we remember the component parts of the leadership drama – the script, the audience, the costume, the plot, the emotional impact, the sense-making – our leadership role will be effective.

We will have to rehearse as well. You might be able to generate the same vitriol and foreboding as Jack Nicholson in *A Few Good Men* when you say, 'you *want* me on that wall ... you *need* me on that wall!'. But, if people think you are just trying to be Colonel Nathan Jessop, or trying to imitate Jack Nicholson, you will lose credibility and following. Be your authentic self, as you live out the role, the script, the costume, the plot, the audience, the emotional impact, and the sense-making. Yes, leadership is drama. Our challenge is to study leadership from the perspective of the social construction of leadership as drama.

Dramatism and dramaturgical analysis have been around for many years. Burke (1975), Turner (1974) and Goffman (1959) were the creators of this field of scholarship, but its incursion into leadership scholarship is more recent. Starratt's (1993) book initiated travel into the area of leadership as drama. Gardner and Avolio (1998) conducted a dramaturgical investigation of the charismatic relationship, which is of course a prominent manifestation of leadership. This is an extremely fertile direction for leadership research.

The aim of this book is certainly not to track through the history of leadership research. Conventional textbooks perform that task well enough. However, having said that, the student can observe a transition over time in the progressive maturity of the world of leadership research. Initially, researchers asked the general question, 'Who is the leader?'. As the answer to that question became progressively more problematic, scholars had a nagging doubt that perhaps they were asking the wrong question. As a general rule, they began to ask another question. They began to ask, 'What does the leader do?'. The interrogation of this question was extremely fruitful, but the nagging doubts came back. It began to become apparent that there was much more to leadership than certain people doing certain things. There were higher purposes at stake and there were dramas unfolding. Consequently, it appeared that other questions were needed. Today, the contemporary research questions revolve around something like, 'What is going on?'. It is this larger processual question of what is going on, as certain people do certain things that have a leadership impact upon other people, which must be teased out and unpacked by researchers.

conclusion

In this chapter we looked at a series of related efforts to rehabilitate and invigorate leadership in response to widespread concerns that were brought into dramatic relief by a number of corporate scandals that erupted in the first part of the twenty-first century. Three rapidly growing areas of leadership scholarship were examined which have sought to respond to the shortcomings of mainstream leadership: ethical leadership, authentic leadership, spiritual leadership. The chapter closed with a consideration of how a more aesthetically-informed approach to leadership might improve our understanding and our practice of leadership, particularly when we look at it through the lens of the arts.

7

Conclusion: Take Your Lead

'Leadership should be aimed at helping to free people from oppressive structures, practices and habits encountered in societies and institutions, as well as within the shady recesses of ourselves. Good leaders liberate. Further, we can liberate leadership thinking itself from its narrow instrumental confines, so it may reconnect with ideals.'

Amanda Sinclair *in Leadership for the Disillusioned* (2007: vx)

The term 'research and development' or 'R & D' is often used to capture that set of activities aimed at identifying and testing new products or services. With respect to the leadership field, 'research' activities have sought better to understand what constitutes good and bad leadership and, in light of this knowledge, make recommendations about how we might promote better leadership. Much of the book has been taken up with explaining to you the range of activities that have been undertaken under the 'research' umbrella. 'Development' activities supposedly take into account that knowledge and create ways in which leadership might be better understood more widely by practitioners and improved through a variety of learning processes and interventions which will be described in this chapter.

In the leadership field, the 'development' part of the R & D equation has tended to take the lion's share of resources in terms of money and time. As we saw in Chapter 1, leadership is big business – these resources are by no means 'small potatoes'. Torn between investing directly into leadership development activities and investing in leadership research, funding gatekeepers – whether they are senior executives or government policy makers – will tend to put their money into leadership development activities, the thinking being that the need to develop leadership talent is an urgent matter which requires immediate attention. Research can wait for another day. Besides, it's hard to see the benefits of research. Development activities are so much more visible and action-oriented.

Consequently, the 'R' part of the R & D activities has become the poorer relation. To a certain extent, leadership researchers might wish to consider shouldering some of the blame for this state of affairs. We have not done as good a job as we might have in selling the benefits of leadership research. In fact, one of the reasons why many of us have opted to engage in leadership development activities is to generate resources that can be invested into funding leadership research.

Of course, the more astute leadership researchers have endeavoured to exploit potential synergies between research and development activities. Leadership development activities create opportunities to engage with leaders who are participating in their programmes. These leaders help to research questions, research priorities and act as sources of data. They also become primary audiences for leadership research, acting as initial sounding boards before research findings are more widely disseminated. This type of synergistic R & D model is the one that we have tried to develop at Excelerator: The New Zealand Leadership Institute and is practised by a number of the other leadership centres throughout the world that we have listed in the Appendix.

A critical element in this R & D strategy is the engagement by senior undergraduate and postgraduate students in leadership projects that are connected to leadership development activities. Along these lines, if this book has done what it was supposed to do and your desire to research leadership has been reinforced (rather than weakened) then we strongly encourage you to think about how you might become more familiar with the leadership development field in general and to become aware of and, if possible, make some connection with leadership development activities that might be taking place in your immediate vicinity.

If you are considering a longer-term career in the leadership field then it is very likely, given what we have said about investment priorities, that you will have to spend some time learning the ropes and becoming an active player in leadership development. Very few leadership researchers do not engage in any form of leadership development. In fact, Brad spent almost ten years in leadership development before he began to conduct his own leadership research. Today he still spends over half of his time engaged in some form of leadership development activity. This not only serves to get him out of the ivory tower but also keeps him plugged into the experiences and preoccupations of leaders from the private, public and not-for-profit sectors. This also provides a ready and useful means to road-test new theories and findings with a view towards receiving a 'reality check'.

For these reasons we will focus this chapter on the 'development' side of the R & D equation. We will briefly look at the range of activities that generally constitute leadership development. We will also consider some of the problems and limitations associated with conventional leadership development activities problems that have been raised by various commentators. Related to this we will discuss some of the recommendations that have been made about how the still very nascent field of leadership development should evolve in the future.

We will close the chapter by considering what you might wish to do, as the next step of your own leadership research journey, by sketching out some areas that you may wish to take a look at.

developing leaders

In his review of the evidence regarding how leaders learn to become leaders, Doh (2003) makes the point that, even if we can learn to lead, it does not mean that leadership can be taught. It is possible that the process of learning is simply too complex, unconscious or non-replicable to teach. His review suggests that some leadership can be learned and some aspects of it can be taught. Jay Conger illustrates this conundrum to graphic effect in his overview of the leadership development process from his book, *Learning to Lead*. He notes:

> The development of leadership ability is a very complex process. It starts before birth, with a prerequisite of certain genes that favour intelligence, physical stamina, and perhaps other qualities. Family members, peers, education, sport, and other childhood experiences then influence the child's need for achievement, power, risk taking and so on. Work experiences and mentors shape the raw leadership materials of childhood and early adulthood into actual leadership by providing essential knowledge and behavioural skills. Opportunity and luck are the final determinants of who gets the chance to lead'. (Conger, 1992: 33)

With respect to the ways in which leaders learn about leadership, most individuals will readily acknowledge that leadership is something that is learned largely and primarily through experience. Unfortunately, there are no short cuts when it comes to experience, although more than a few popular business book writers have endeavoured to claim this is possible. Experience is not something that can be speeded up but it's clear that some experiences can be managed in such a way that leaders can gain more insight and knowledge (McCall and Lombardo, 1988). Several studies have shown that learning from experience is affected by the amount of challenge, the variety of task or assignments, and the quality of feedback that is received by the participants.

Challenges that are given to developing leaders need to enable the participants to experience success as well as failure (assuming the person accepts responsibility for this). These challenges should not engender excessive stress and strain. It is especially beneficial for managers to have early experience with a wide variety of problems that require different leadership behaviours and skills. However, it is also important for developing leaders to stick with a task or project long enough to see and reflect upon the consequences, favourable or otherwise, of their actions as a leader. Too often in this fast-paced world we move on before we have the chance to see the real and lasting impact of our work as leaders – good, bad or negligible. Useful feedback about a leader's behaviour is seldom provided within operational assignments, and even when it is available, it may not result in learning due to a combination of a lack of time and reticence on the part of the leaders and followers to either give or receive feedback.

on-the-job leadership development

With respect to the kinds of leadership development activity that can be used to facilitate the learning of relevant leadership skills on the job, Yukl (2002) identifies the following seven activities as being the most widely used.

Multi-source feedback (e.g. '360-degree' feedback and 'multi-rater' feedback such as the MLQ that we discussed in Chapter 2)   This tends to be expensive, time-consuming and better suited to large organizations, not small organizations. A relatively recent innovation, the jury is still out on how effective this form of feedback really is in developing leadership.

Development Assessment Centres   Traditionally geared to selection and promotion decisions, there has been a growing interest in using these centres to develop managers. As with multi-source feedback, development centres are expensive, time-consuming, and their effectiveness has not been established in the literature.

Developmental Assignments   This includes being assigned to specific projects, different parts of the organization, or suppliers or customers of the organization. Job rotation is a process by which managers are assigned to work in a variety of different functional sub-units of an organization for periods of time varying from six months to three years. There is the danger that a person could be moved too quickly with insufficient time to see the consequences of their actions or reflect on the experience. Staying in the position too long can lead to boredom and lost opportunities for more meaningful development.

Action learning   Individuals or teams conduct field projects on complex organizational problems requiring the use of skills learned on formal training sessions. The emphasis is on developing cognitive and interpersonal skills rather than technical knowledge. The effectiveness of action learning is dependent upon the type of project, the composition of the team and the type of coaching required.

Mentoring   This is a relationship in which a more experienced leader helps a less experienced protégé. Mentors provide a psychosocial function (e.g. acceptance, encouragement, etc.) as well as a career-facilitation function (e.g. sponsorship, protection, exposure, etc.). The success of formal mentoring programmes is probably increased by making participation voluntary, providing mentors with a choice of protégé, by explaining the benefits and pitfalls and clarifying expectations, roles and processes of mentor and protégé to both parties.

Executive Coaching   This has experienced a rapid increase in popularity. Coaching is usually provided to a high-level executive by either a successful former executive or a management consultant. It has several advantages over formal training programmes: convenience, confidentiality, flexibility, and more personal attention. However, it is very expensive and good coaches are hard to find.

Outdoor Challenge Programmes These involve physical activities performed by a group of people in an outdoor setting. Participants are given a sequence of increasingly challenging activities that require mutual trust and co-operation among group members. Limited research evaluation has been conducted on the effectiveness of this type of programme, although generally much fun is had by all. Results to date have been inconsistent regarding its effectiveness in promoting leadership.

formal leadership training

Most leadership training programmes are designed to increase generic skills and behaviours that are relevant for leadership effectiveness and advancement. The old pattern (affectionately referred to as 'sheep dipping' in the trade) of selecting mostly 'fast-track' managers for leadership training and providing it only once or twice during a manager's career is gradually being replaced by a series of leadership training opportunities that are available to any manager in the organization at appropriate points in her or his career (Yukl, 2002).

It's important to recognize that you cannot *train* leaders. You can, however, help to develop certain behaviours and skills that can assist individuals in leading others. Training in interpersonal communication skills, presentation skills, decision-making skills and facilitation skills can be very helpful. But these are merely means to an end. Many leaders have got by without fully (or, in some cases, even partially) developing these skills. What's really important is the ability continually to learn from your experiences. Education can play a part here in that it can provide us with new and challenging ways of looking and conceptualizing our and others' experiences. But, like training, it's better treated as a means not an end to leadership development. It also needs to be situated in a planned and integrated model of leadership development (Cacioppe, 1998). Generally an unreasonable expectation is placed on the specific training programme to make the radical changes that might be required when, in fact, individuals spend so little of their time participating in these activities compared to their 'real work'.

A large variety of methods are used for leadership training. When we design leadership training programmes, we tend to bring together a blend of instructional approaches that takes into account the different learning preferences of those who are participating in the programme and the need to keep the learning process dynamic and engaging. We especially find that mixing short 'lecturettes' and small group and large group discussion – combined with experiential exercises, case studies and role modelling – tends to work most effectively with a wide range of audiences. The case studies can take both written and visual form but are generally more effective when they are directly relevant to the participants' direct experience and are processed initially in small groups and then debriefed in large groups. Role modelling can either involve guest speakers who have successfully led not-for-profit organizations or involve role-playing in typical leadership situations. Other teaching methods that we have found to be useful include psychometric tests, site visits, and participant role plays and presentations.

With respect to selecting the most appropriate training programmes, you should look for a programme that has stood the test of time. Avoid programmes that emphasize the latest and greatest techniques. Leadership is an ancient art – in truth, not that much has changed despite what the hype suggests. So, it is important to ask: what kind of a track record does this programme have? Can you talk to alumni of the programme from both the recent and more distant past? To what extent has the facilitator had a stake in the development of the programme? Have they just been booked in to the lead the session?

Along the same lines, it is important to steer away from programmes that promise you instant or substantial results. Leadership is not something that is won so easily or so convincingly. It is something that has to be constantly worked at, day in, day out; it's also something that can be lost more quickly than it is gained. While, in the interests of persuading individuals to sign up for a programme, it is tempting to make bold claims about a programme, it is irresponsible for any trainer to make this claim when, for 50 per cent of every training programme, the onus is on the individual who participates in the training. Ask yourself, how hard are you willing to work at developing your leadership potential? Is it the right time for you to undertake this type of training? Do you really want it, and why?

the problem with leadership development

As we saw in the opening chapter, leadership development has become a multibillion global industry. Grint provides estimates of between $15 and $50 billion annually for the world (Grint, 2007). Despite these staggering sums, many commentators argue that this is not sufficient given the range and scope of leadership challenges faced by humanity. For example, Jay Conger asserts that, 'most would agree that to seriously train individuals in the arts of leadership takes enormous time and resources – perhaps more than societies or organisations possess, and certainly more than they are willing to expend' (1992: 73).

Surprisingly, given the amount of money that is invested in leadership development, very little has been done to evaluate the impact of this investment (Dvir et al., 2002). Much of what has been written has been generated by trainers or consultants who often have a vested interest in promoting their particular leadership programme or intervention. The research that has attempted to do just this has by no means been definitive in its evaluation of the effectiveness of leadership development. Moreover, it has not been able to isolate what types of leadership development are most effective.

In general, individuals who participate in leadership development programmes tend to be clearer and more positive about leadership development programmes than the organizations that sponsor them. Most corporate leaders who are responsible for management and leadership development programmes see it as an act of faith: it is better to do the development work than risk the consequences of not doing it.

Researchers have long highlighted the need for more empirical studies that examine managerial leadership development (Brungardt, 1996; Collins, 2001a; Day, 2000; Lynham, 2000), but still these calls have remained largely unheeded. Transformational leadership is also represented strongly in published work on leadership development. For example, a study conducted by Ken and Paresha Sinha found that the display of transformational leadership by people in leadership positions increased with two days' interaction and three months' application back at work. Using a quasi field-experiment they found increases in all five transformational leadership behaviours and contingent reward behaviour, and decreases in display of passive transactional leadership behaviour, as a result of the training. Followers put in an increased amount of observable extra effort. Goal-setting was also found to be a particularly effective learning intervention method (Parry and Sinha, 2005).

Virtually all the work on leadership development is conducted at the individual level of analysis. More specifically, it looks at how to increase levels of leadership skills within individual leaders. There is a major need for research into how to develop the processes of sharing leadership, either as co-leadership or in a more distributed form as we discussed in Chapter 5. There is also a need for research into leadership development at a collective level either within a team or throughout an entire organization. The full range of methodologies is available here. There are opportunities for questionnaire research, as always. This work could be complemented by more experimental work. There are opportunities for work on assessment centres by human resource management researchers. There is also wide scope for more case studies of an ethnographic nature.

Of course, training people to be better leaders will be all for nought unless the environment within which they operate is conducive to allowing that type of leadership to flourish. Another study conducted by Ken, this time with Sarah Proctor-Thomson, showed quite clearly that the leadership displayed by individuals is strongly moderated by the culture, climate and bureaucratization of the work environment (Parry and Proctor-Thomson, 2003). There is no real surprise here, but the point is that much more work must be done into how the working environment moderates the impact of leadership on the performance of the organization. Leadership training and development will be useless if the deep power structures reinforce existing leadership hierarchies that constrain progressive forms of leadership (Gordon, 2002).

developing leadership for the future

We do have some concerns that in developing the next generation of leaders we may have made the assumption that their desire to lead will occur as a matter of course, as it did for our generation. Our experience in working with undergraduate and postgraduate students, who are likely to contribute heavily to the pool of future leaders, is that they are ambivalent about taking on the responsibilities and pressures associated with leading organizations. Or perhaps it is the case that they are concerned that, in order to lead these organizations, they will have to lead them in ways they are uncomfortable with on ideological or philosophical grounds. They have seen what the current leaders have to endure, in terms of an increasingly invasive and highly cynical public that is looking to its leaders to perform miracles and disparages them if they fall short.

As we saw from our discussion of the romance of leadership in Chapter 3, these challenges have always been a fact of life for leaders but it is arguable that the pressures to succeed have never been as pronounced as they are today. Naturally, many individuals whom we would have expected to aspire to leadership are not as willing to seek out leadership positions and make the necessary sacrifices. Potentially we may have to face a major leadership aspiration problem throughout the world. This is something that leadership development must actively take into account.

In the past when we have endeavoured to develop leaders we have tended to focus our attention on cognitive understanding (i.e. *knowing* leadership). To a lesser extent we have also devoted some effort and attention to developing a behavioural understanding of leadership (i.e. *acting* leadership). What we really need to understand and foster are the emotional aspects of leadership (i.e. *feeling* leadership). Frequently, when you look at leadership failure, it comes down to emotional issues not cognitive behavioural ones. Most specifically, does the leader have sufficient emotional toughness or resilience to survive the tough times? The notion of 'Emotional Intelligence' (EI) that has been popularized by Daniel Goleman has something important to offer leaders in that it brings into consideration the emotional realm that the leadership field has sorely missed. Goleman (1998) has argued that having high levels of emotional intelligence is important to leaders because it enables them to better adapt to different situations, especially crises; it also enables them to better understand their own emotional needs and those of their followers. In addition, through stronger self-regulation, emotionally intelligent leaders are able to maintain a positive frame of mind even when many around them have strong negative feelings about the situation.

Almost all leadership development activities are aimed at those who occupy or are about to occupy formal leadership roles. If we re-cognize that leadership is co-produced, would it not make sense to extend leadership development activities to include followers as well as leaders? Day (2000) has helpfully distinguished between a 'leader development' orientation which focuses on developing the individual capabilities of leaders (i.e. building 'human capital') and 'leadership development' which focuses on developing reciprocal relations and commitments (i.e. building 'social capital'). Currently, far too much emphasis is being placed on the former rather than the latter (Drath, 2001). What is generically referred to as leadership development is, in fact, leader development. Jones (2005) notes that current leadership development programmes can perpetuate leaders' self-preoccupations through their emphasis on 'self-development', 'self-awareness' and 'self-improvement' at the expense of understanding their followers.

A key challenge of effective leadership development should, therefore, be to develop a more sophisticated understanding of what it means to be a good follower as well as a good leader. We have developed a reasonably robust understanding of the different types of leader, but we still tend to treat followers as a homogeneous entity. We therefore need a way of thinking about leadership development which 'views the identities of followers and leaders as inextricably linked, mutually reinforcing, and shifting within specific contexts' (Collinson, 2006: 187).

In contrast to our traditional orientation toward leader–follower relations which considers relations from the standpoint of individuals as independent, discrete entities, this 'relational' view of leadership starts with processes, and views persons and leadership as things that are made through these processes (Hosking, 2007). Leadership development and training should not only include both leaders and followers, but should actively blur the leader–follower divide, generate a collective understanding, and resist the temptation to impose top-down predefined models of leadership in favour of bottom-up locally generated content. In this regard we need to create more 'cultured' leadership development programmes.

Andrew Jones has raised some interesting anthropological questions about the nature and purpose of leadership development programmes across cultures. In evaluating a number of the world's most prestigious leadership development programmes, he argues that, in addition to the work of 'developing individual leaders' to make their sponsoring organizations more effective, the leadership development process also serves an important role as a context for organizations and cultures to confront and (attempt to) resolve social and economic conflicts affecting the larger society as well. Drawing on the language of symbolic anthropology, he sees leadership development programmes as sites of 'ritual process' through which executives grapple with moral and ethical matters through self-reflection (Jones, 2006). In other words, leadership development programmes frequently provide an opportunity for leaders to work through leadership issues which are well beyond the organizations that they are immediately associated with and which have footed the bill for the programme.

A useful guide as to how we might make these 'cultured' leadership programmes as useful and generative as possible has been provided by Amanda Sinclair. She has written passionately about her concerns regarding the current state of leadership development and leadership education which she observes as being preoccupied by heroic, leader-centric notions of leadership (described in Chapter 2) that ultimately serve to disempower both leaders and followers – and, in so doing, preserve the status quo. As you saw from the opening quote to this chapter, Amanda wants to promote leadership development that will not imprison but liberate leaders to think about new and creative ways to lead.

In her recently published book which is provocatively entitled *Leadership for the Disillusioned* she talks about her own struggle to make her teaching more impactful and more liberating. She now incorporates three principles into all of her leadership teaching. First, reflection has become the basis for learning to become a better leader. Students are encouraged to dig deep into their own history, investigating their own path as a leader and as a follower. Second, learning comes from direct experience. The class itself becomes the primary source of leadership learning. Finally, leadership theory is used as a body of ideas and concepts which is to be examined critically in light of the participants' experiences but also on ethical and moral grounds. This is something that we both strongly subscribe to. Indeed we hope the book you are currently reading has presented the various leadership theories in such a way that it has encouraged you to engage critically with these theories not take them as gospel. At the end of the day we judge the quality of a leadership theory by the quality of the questions it creates in our minds rather than the quality of the answers that it gives.

Sinclair's approach to teaching leadership is backed up by another leading leadership educator, Keith Grint, who has suggested that we can fruitfully return to Aristotle's division between Techné (skills), Episteme (knowledge) and Phronesis (wisdom) in an effort to understand whether or not leadership can be taught and, if so, why some aspects seem so difficult to teach. He concludes that although leadership educators may be able to teach skills and knowledge directly, wisdom, which is fundamentally important to leadership effectiveness, is something that can be achieved only through reflective experience of learning. In light of this we should be concentrating on the construction of opportunities to lead rather than on the selection of leaders, the construction of competency frameworks or the use of formal lectures. He underlines his argument by closing his paper with the poem by Piet Hein called 'The Road to Wisdom' which reads as follow: 'the road to wisdom – well, it's plain and simple to express: err and err and err again but less and less and less'.

A corollary of this approach is that 'perhaps the first step is for those involved in the education of leaders to acquire more humility concerning the limits of their experience' (Grint, 2007: 18). This is something that Ken and Brad have no trouble getting to grips with our family, colleagues and students certainly make sure of that.

developing future leadership researchers

This book has endeavoured to give you a quick, yet reasonably comprehensive idea of the range of things that leadership scholars are interested in researching as well as some indication as to *how* they go about researching these phenomena. We hope that at least one and perhaps a number of the areas that we have reviewed has sparked your interest and got you thinking about how you might become more involved in studying leadership.

Ideally, of course, we hope you are feeling like us: slightly overwhelmed by the range of possible leadership topics that you'd like to study. If this is the case, then you're well on your way to becoming a leadership scholar. With respect to coping with this feeling, the wisest advice Brad ever received from one of his earlier mentors was to draw up a notional twenty-year research programme with three columns. The first column is for those projects you want to pursue within the near future (i.e. within the next one to three years). The second column contains those projects you want to work on in the medium term (say three to ten years). The third column holds those projects that you want to get to in the longer term (i.e. ten to twenty years). Of course, you are never likely to get to any of these in the third column, but at least you have the feeling that you haven't dropped them.

With respect to what leadership topic you might choose to focus on in the near future, consider thinking about a leadership issue that has affected you personally, whether it is something that has happened to you as a follower or as a leader. This might be something that has happened to you in a direct, face-to-face leader–follower relationship or it might be something that you have observed through the media or read historic accounts of. Usually, if a fundamental spark of interest is generated – either through annoyance or anger, or through respect or admiration – it's a good sign that you might be on to something. In our preliminary conversations with students who are thinking about doing leadership research, we talk to them about their experiences and listen carefully for cues as to what moves them personally. Invariably, this is manifested in a speeding up or increased animation in their voices.

For example, an Indonesian student whom Brad supervised talked about his experience working for a manager who had been brought in to run the planning department in which he worked. In a very short time, thanks to the manager's inspiring leadership, the department changed from being a very slow, moribund and sleepy outpost of the company to a dynamic, vibrant and growing concern that many were queuing up to join. This student was mystified because within three months, despite this remarkable turnaround, his manager was unceremoniously fired. Brad encouraged the student to go back to the company as a researcher to find out what had happened from the perspective of a number of observers within and outside the company. The thesis provided the student with a number of invaluable lessons regarding the finer arts of upward leadership, as well as longer-term survival strategies within complex organizations.

Once you have an idea of the topic or research problem that you want to focus on, it's time to think about how you might go about researching it. A useful exercise here is to think about how each of the perspectives that we have discussed in this book – either leader-centric, follower-centric, culturally, critically or spiritually-oriented perspectives – might look at and position your research problem. There is a tendency, in the interests of expediency, to pigeonhole a research problem too early in the process, to take the most obvious lens on the problem either because it's the one you are the most familiar with or because everybody else is doing it. If you take this line, you are more than likely to prematurely shut out some potentially creative options which might, in the long run, yield fresher and ultimately more profound insights into your problem.

Brad recalls, having decided that he was going to focus on management gurus and what lay behind their extraordinary appeal, that he 'tried on' many different research methodologies as you would try on pairs of shoes in a shoe store. In this case he veered dangerously close to Imelda Marcos territory. A useful technique in this regard is to generate many different 'proto' projects, dissertations or theses in the manner of directors who generate 'movie pitches'. It was in the course of generating one of these prototypes that he discovered, in one of those all too rare 'ah-ah' moments, that the peculiarly named Fantasy Theme Analysis was going to get at exactly what he wanted to examine in his thesis. The next challenge, of course, was to persuade his sceptical supervisor that this method was the way to go.

With respect to coming up with a research design, that is working out who will you will approach and with what means, it is extremely useful to look at model pieces of empirical work. In this book we have tried to give you a flavour of the range of research methods that are used in leadership research by providing brief descriptions of sample empirical studies. These have included questionnaire surveys, laboratory experiments, document analyses, discourse analyses and participant-observation. We advise you to track down some of the studies we have referred to and examine in detail how they designed their empirical research projects and how they structured their accounts of them. You can learn a lot from both their successes and their failures. Sometimes, merely replicating what they have done in your own empirical context is a sufficiently valuable contribution to leadership knowledge.

To this end, we strongly advise you to conduct a small pilot study to experiment with a particular method before launching headlong into a major study. One thing you will appreciate very early on is that conducting original research is a lot trickier than you imagined before you embarked upon it. You will quickly gain a greater appreciation for the research that has been done. On a more positive note, it's a lot more personally rewarding than you could ever imagine.

Essentially our best advice is to determine your research problem fairly early on in the process but to give yourself plenty of time to choose from a variety of ways in which you might go about investigating the problem. Be prepared to read widely and explore more than a few blind alleys. Remember, no exploration is ever wasted. It is likely to serve you well in the future, especially when it comes time to defend your work.

The good news, as we said at the outset, is that there has never been so much interest or support for doing leadership research. You will have no trouble explaining to a potential research participant why your research is important or significant. Besides, everyone wants to talk about leadership. It's something that everyone has an opinion on and most people are keen to share these opinions. Research subjects will, therefore, invariably be keen to assist you as long as you respect their busy schedule and, of course, their privacy.

The privacy issue highlights one of the challenges that are particularly salient to leadership researchers. When talking to leaders, it is sometimes quite difficult to determine what they really think about a particular aspect of leadership. There will be a tendency either to want to tell you what they think you want to hear about leadership or to convey a good impression about their leadership. Because we live in a society that places such great stock in being an effective leader, it is difficult for leaders to talk about where they might come up short. Somewhat perversely, it might be more acceptable to admit to one or two weaknesses as a manager but never as a leader. Of course this is less of a problem for followers, many of whom will freely lay most of their personal woes and injustices at the foot of their leader.

Moreover, there is high potential for confusion about whether a subject is talking about how they would *ideally* like to lead or be led and how they *actually* lead or are led. Of course, the higher you go in the organization, the more this is likely to be the case – simply because the stakes are a lot higher. Exposing how one leads not only has the potential to adversely affect the reputation of the leader but also the reputation of the company or organization they lead. Of course, the leader and the company's reputation can be considerably enhanced if a favourable portrayal of leadership can be conveyed. To counter this problem, considerable investment needs to be put into building sufficient levels of trust with research subjects to enable the researcher to get at these issues.

The pressures exerted by thesis submission, publishing or promotion deadlines, mean that researchers often do not have the luxury of time to conduct this kind of deep research. One response is to focus on leaders at the lower levels within a company where access and cooperation might be more readily secured. This is why there is a relative dearth in senior-level leadership research, when it is sorely needed.

Another response to time pressures is to select research methods that are comparatively efficient, reliable and widely accepted. For this reason the survey and the laboratory experiment continue to be the preferred research methods of choice for many leadership researchers rather than ethnographically-rooted participant-observation which requires considerably more time and presents greater risks. It's also why so much leadership research is conducted either on students or within the university or other educational settings. Those who are willing to spend the time, look further afield and take risks, are rewarded by the fact that invariably their studies will become heavily cited and respected because they have endeavoured to get in among those who practise leadership and management in a more than superficial way. Good examples of these types of studies would be Rosabeth Moss Kanter's *Men and Women of the Corporation* (1977), Robert

Jackall's *Moral Mazes* (1988), Gideon Kunda's *Manufacturing Consent* (1992) and Tony Watson's *In Search of Management* (1994).

With respect to writing up your research and disseminating to others your hard-won and precious leadership knowledge, we suggest that you again 'look and learn' from the more experienced and seasoned researchers who can provide you with exemplars to work from. To this end, we have dared to compile in the Appendix a list of 'Ten Leadership Books That You Should Read Before You Die'. Read these books not only for what they say about leadership but *how* they write about leadership. In a similar way to musicians, actively try to mimic these styles. They will start to rub off on your own writing.

Another tip: when you track these books down in your library, look either side of them on the shelf and grab four or five of their less famous neighbouring books and flick through their contents, introductory and concluding chapters. You'll be amazed what you will discover. You will also start to see some recurring themes that will give you the confidence that you are starting to 'get' leadership. In the age of instant access to knowledge provided by electronic database searching technology, we have lost the art of semi-random browsing which spending real time in libraries still affords, yet students and academics now rarely take advantage of.

Doing any kind of undergraduate or postgraduate study is like serving a form of apprenticeship. To be honest, in academe, the apprenticeship is effectively a life sentence because you can never truly master your subject – especially when it is something as nebulous, as contestable and as fascinating as leadership. The academics we most admire are those who still consider themselves to be students. They are as excited and as mind-boggled by their subject as they were when they started out on their studies, as hopefully you are right now. Their research, their teaching and their service activities all work together to help them become more accomplished students of leadership. Every waking moment of their day presents them with an opportunity to learn something more about leadership, for which they are constantly grateful. Be warned, though: like the infamous 'Hotel California', you can check in any time to study leadership but you can never check out.

conclusion

Looking back to what we said we wanted to achieve in this book under the heading 'Should you Buy this Book?' we hoped that, if you were already a university student studying leadership or perhaps contemplating studying leadership as part of a senior undergraduate or a postgraduate course, this book might provide an excellent base from which to proceed. You should have gained a 'quick and dirty' feel for what gets studied within leadership and how it gets studied. It's possible, of course, that the book might have confirmed your worst suspicions about the field of leadership being 'fuzzy and flaky' and you have firmly decided that it is not for you. In that case, your investment in this book has been a sound one.

For those of you who are on the verge of starting a project, dissertation or thesis on leadership, we hope that you not only have an even better handle on the various ways that you might go about doing this but you feel affirmed in your choice to join the field of leadership studies. We hope we have encouraged you to select a research problem that is not only important to you personally but has some general significance that we can all benefit from. We also urge you to be creative and innovative in your research design and to take risks with your research, but heed well the lessons of experience that your supervisors will pass on to you.

Because this is such a young and growing field, you have every opportunity to play an active role in building knowledge about leadership and making your mark. In this regard you are by no means alone. We, therefore, strongly encourage you to join the groups of leadership researchers and developers that we have listed in the Appendix; come to the conferences and get involved in reviewing and writing for leadership journals, both for practitioners and academic audiences. On the local front, either find or found a local special-interest group that shares your passion and fascination for leadership.

For those of you who are not currently engaged in a formal programme of study but have always had an interest in leadership, we hope you have been encouraged or perhaps have even inspired to 'promptly march down to your nearest seat of learning and sign up for a formal programme to find others who have already decided to make that fateful leap'. While our tongues are firmly implanted in our cheeks when we make this statement, we do want to underline the well-worn cliché that 'there is no time like the present' to pursue your studies. We both embarked on our doctoral studies in our mid-thirties when families and careers were at their most demanding, yet we never once regretted taking that step. It opened up a whole new world of learning for us which, in this book, we've striven to share with you.

Finally, for those of our academic colleagues who are not involved in leadership research or have always been mildly suspicious of it, we hope that reading this book has served to at least partially allay your suspicions and may have even whetted your appetite to explore leadership studies even further. In our wildest evangelical dreams, we speculate that a few of you may have come to the realization that you are, after all, already doing leadership research and are now willing to 'come out of the closet'. To you we say 'be brave' and 'amen'. There will be those who, as a result of reading this book, might have become scandalized by what passes for leadership research and are moved to shut down all leadership research centres forthwith. To you we say: 'catch you later'.

References

Adler, N.J. (1996) 'Global women political leaders: An invisible history, and increasingly important future', *Leadership Quarterly*, 7 (1): 133–61.

Ailon-Souday, G. and Kunda, G. (2003) 'The local selves of global workers: The social construction of national identity in the face of organizational globalization', *Organization Studies*, 24 (7): 1073–96.

Alimo-Metcalfe, B. and Alban-Metcalfe, R.J. (2001) 'The development of a new Transformational Leadership Questionnaire', *Journal of Occupational and Organizational Psychology*, 74: 1–28.

Alvarez, J.L. and Svejenova, S. (2005) *Sharing Executive Power*. Cambridge: Cambridge University Press.

Alvesson, M. (1993) *Cultural Perspectives on Organization*. Cambridge: Cambridge University Press.

Alvesson, M. and Sveningsson, S. (2003) 'The great disappearing act: Difficulties in doing "leadership"', *Leadership Quarterly*, 14 (3): 359–81.

Astin, H.S. and Leland, C. (1992) *Women of Influence, Women of Vision: A Cross-Generational Study of Leaders and Social Change*. San Francisco, CA: Jossey-Bass.

Avolio, B. (2005) *Leadership Development in Balance: MADE/Born*. Mahwah, NJ: LEA.

Avolio, B. and Bass, B. (1995) 'Individual consideration viewed at multiple levels of analysis: A multi-level framework for examining the diffusion of transformational leadership', *Leadership Quarterly*, 6 (2): 199–218.

Avolio, B.J., Bass, B.M. and Jung, D.I. (1999a) 'Re-examining the components of transformational and transactional leadership using the multifactor leadership questionnaire', *Journal of Occupational and Organizational Psychology*, 72: 441–62.

Avolio, B.J., Howell, J.M. and Sosik, J.J. (1999b) 'A funny thing happened on the way to the bottom line: Humor as a moderator of leadership style effects', *Academy of Management Journal*, 42 (2): 219–27.

Avolio, B.J., Kahai, S. and Dodge, G.E. (2001) 'E-Leadership: Implications for theory, research, and practice', *Leadership Quarterly*, 11 (4): 615–68.

Avolio, B.J., Sivasubramaniam, N., Murry, W.D., Jung, D. and Garger, J.W. (2003) 'Assessing shared leadership: Development and preliminary validation of a team multifactor leadership questionnaire', in C.L. Pearce and J.A Conger (eds), *Shared Leadership: Reframing the Hows and Whys of Leadership*. Thousand Oaks, CA: Sage. pp. 143–72.

Awamleh, R. and Gardner, W.L. (1999) 'Perceptions of leaders charisma and effectiveness: The effects of vision content, delivery, and organizational performance', *Leadership Quarterly*, 10 (3): 345–73.

Babiak, P. (1996) 'Psychopathic manipulation in organizations: Pawns, patrons, and patsies', in D.J. Cooke, A.E. Forth, J.P. Newman and R.D. Hare (eds), *Issues in Criminological and Legal Psychology: No. 24, International Perspectives on Psychopathy*. Leicester, UK: British Psychological Society, pp. 12–17.

Badaracco, J.L. (2002) *Leading Quietly: An Unorthodox Guide to Doing the Right Thing*. Boston, MA: Harvard Business Press.

Banker, R.D., Field, J.M., Schroeder, R.G. and Sinha, K.K. (1996) 'Impact of work teams on manufacturing performance: A longitudinal field study', *Academy of Management Journal*, 39: 867–90.

Barker, J.R. (1993) 'Tightening the iron cage: Concertive control in self-managing teams', *Administrative Science Quarterly*, 38 (3): 408–37.

Barnard, C.I. (1938) *The Functions of the Executive*. Cambridge, MA: Harvard University Press.

Bass, B.M. (1985) *Leadership and Performance Beyond Expectations*. New York: Free Press.

Bass, B.M. (1990) 'Concepts of leadership', in B.M. Bass and R.M. Stodgill's *Handbook of Leadership: Theory, Research and Managerial Applications*. New York: Free Press.

Bass, B.M. (1997) 'Does the transactional and transformational leadership paradigm transcend organizational and national boundaries?', *American Psychologist*, 52 (2): 130–9.

Bass, B.M. (1998) *Transformational Leadership: Industrial, Military and Educational Impact*. Mahwah, NJ: Lawrence Erlbaum.

Bass, B.M. and Avolio, B.J. (1990) 'The implications of transactional and transformational leadership for individual, team, and organizational development', *Research in Organizational Change and Development*, 4: 231–72.

Bass, B.M. and Avolio, B.J. (1994) 'Shatter the glass ceiling: Women may make better managers', *Human Resource Management*, 33: 549–60.

Bass, B.M. and Steidlmeier, P. (1999) 'Ethics, character, and authentic transformational leadership behaviour', *Leadership Quarterly*, 10 (2): 181–217.

Bennis, W.G. and Nanus, B. (1985) *Leaders: the Strategies for Taking Charge*. New York: Harper & Row.

Berson, Y. and Avolio, B. (2004) 'Transformational leadership and the dissemination of organizational goals: A case study of a telecommunication firm', *Leadership Quarterly*, 15 (5): 625–46.

Bhaskar, R. (1989) *Reclaiming Reality: A Critical Introduction to Contemporary Philosophy*. London: Verso.

Boal, K.B. and Hooijberg, R. (2000) 'Strategic leadership research: Moving on', *Leadership Quarterly*, 11 (4), 515–49.

Boje, D.M. (2001) *Narrative Methods for Organizational and Communication Research*. Thousand Oaks, CA: Sage.

Bolman, L.G. and Deal, T.E. (1997) *Reframing Organizations*. San Francisco, CA: Jossey-Bass.

Bratton, J., Grint, K. and Nelson, D.L. (2004) *Organizational Leadership*. New York: Thomson.

Brown, M.E. and Gioia, D.A. (2002) 'Making things click: Distributive leadership in an online division of an offline organization', *Leadership Quarterly*, 13 (4): 397–419.

Brungardt, C. (1996) 'The making of leaders: A review of the research in leadership development and education', *The Journal of Leadership Studies,* 3 (3): 81–95.

Buchanan, D. and Huczynski, A. (2006) *Organizational Behaviour: An Introductory Text*, 6th edn. Harlow, Essex: FT Prentice-Hall.

Burgoyne, J. (2004) 'How certain are we that management and leadership development is effective?'. Paper presented at the Management Learning and Leadership Workshop, Lancaster University, July.

Burke, K. (1975) 'The five key terms of Dramatism', in D. Brissett and C. Edgley (eds), *Life as Theater: A Dramaturgical Sourcebook*. Chicago: Aldine, pp. 445–52.

Burns, J.M. (1978) *Leadership*. New York: Harper & Row.

Burns, J.M. (2003) *Transforming Leadership: A New Pursuit of Leadership*. New York: Atlantic Monthly Press.

Burns, J.M. (2005) 'Leadership', *Leadership*, 1 (1), 11–12.

Cable, D.M. and Judge, T.A. (2003) 'Managers' upward influence tactic strategies: The role of manager personality and supervisor leadership style', *Journal of Organizational Behaviour*, 24 (2): 197–214.

Cacioppe, R. (1998) 'An integrated model and approach for the design of effective leadership programmes', *Leadership and Organization Development Journal*, 19 (1): 44–53.

Calás, M.B. and Smircich, L. (1997) 'Voicing seduction to silence leadership', in K. Grint (ed), *Leadership: Classical, Contemporary and Critical Approaches*. Oxford: Oxford University Press.

Calder, B.J. (1977) 'An attribution theory of leadership', in B.M. Staw and G.R. Salancik (eds), *New Directions in Organizational Behaviour*. Chicago: St Clair, pp. 179–204.

Cammock, P. (2002) *The Dance of Leadership*. Auckland, NZ: Prentice-Hall.

Chatman, J.A. and O'Reilly, C.A. (2004) 'Asymmetric reactions to work group sex diversity among men and women', *Academy of Management Journal*, 47 (2): 193–208.

Chen, C.C. and Meindl, J.R. (1991) 'The construction of leadership images in the popular press: The case of Donald Burr and People Express', *Administrative Science Quarterly*, 36: 521–55.

Christensen, R.A. (1991) 'A personal perspective on tribal Alaska native gifted and talented education', *Journal of American Indian Education*, 31 (1): 10–14.

Cohen, S.G. and Ledford, G.E. (1994) 'The effectiveness of self-managing teams: A field experiment', *Human Relations*, 47: 13–43.

Collins, D.B. (2001) 'Organizational Performance : The future focus of leadership development programs', *The Journal of Leadership Studies,* 7 (4): 43–54.

Collins, J. (2001a) *Good to Great: Why Some Companies Make the Leap ... and Others Don't*. New York: HarperCollins.

Collins, J. (2001b) 'Level 5 leadership: the triumph of humility and fierce resolve', *Harvard Business Review*, 79 (1): 67–76.

Collins, J. and Porras, J.I. (1995) *Built to Last: Successful Habits of Visionary Companies*. New York: HarperCollins.

Collinson, D. (2005) 'Dialectics of leadership', *Human Relations*, 58 (11): 1419–1442.

Collinson, D. (2006) 'Rethinking followership: A post-structuralist analysis of follower identities', *Leadership Quarterly,* 17 (2): 179–89.

Conger, J.A. (1989) *The Charismatic Leader: Behind the Mystique of Exceptional Leadership*. San Francisco, CA: Jossey-Bass.

Conger, J. (1992) *Learning to Lead: The Art of Transforming Managers into Leaders*. San Francisco, CA: Jossey-Bass.

Conger, J.A. (1996) 'The dark side of leadership', in R.M. Steers, L.W. Porter and G.A. Bigley (eds), *Motivation and Leadership at Work,* 6th edn. New York: McGraw-Hill, pp. 658–71.

Conger, J. and Kanungo, R. (1987) 'Toward a behavioral theory of charismatic leadership in organizational settings', *Academy of Management Review*, 12: 637–47.

Cordery, J.L., Mueller, W.S. and Smith, L.M. (1991) 'Attitudinal and behavioural effects of autonomous group working: A longitudinal field study', *Academy of Management Journal*, 34: 464–76.

Craig, S.B. and Gustafson, S.B. (1998) 'Perceived leader integrity scale: An instrument for assessing employee perceptions of leader integrity', *Leadership Quarterly*, 9 (2): 127–45.

Dansereau, F. and Yammarino, F.J. (2006) 'Is more discussion about levels of analysis really necessary? When is such discussion sufficient?', *Leadership Quarterly*, 17 (5): 537–52.

Day, D.V. (2000) 'Leadership development: A review in context', *Leadership Quarterly* 11 (4): 581–613.

Day, D., Gronn, P. and Salas, E. (2004) 'Leadership capacity in teams', *Leadership Quarterly*, 15 (6): 857–80.

Deal, T.E. and Kennedy, A.A. (1982) *Corporate Cultures: The Rites and Rituals of Corporate Life*. New York: Addison-Wesley.

Den Hartog, D.N. and Dickson, M.W. (2004) 'Leadership and Culture' in J. Antonakis, A.T. Cianciolo and R.J. Sternberg (eds), *The Nature of Leadership*. London: Sage, pp. 249–78.

Den Hartog, D.N., Van Muijen, J.J. and Koopman, P.L. (1997) 'Transactional versus transformational leadership: An analysis of the MLQ', *Journal of Occupational and Organizational Psychology*, 70 (1): 19.

Den Hartog, D.N., House, R.J., Hanges, P.J., Ruiz-Quintanilla, S.A., Dorfman, P.W., Field, R.H.G. et al. (1999) 'Culture specific and cross culturally generalizable implicit leadership theories: Are attributes of charismatic/transformational leadership universally endorsed?', *Leadership Quarterly*, 10 (2): 219–56.

Dickson, M.W., Den Hartog, D. and Mitchelson, J. (2003) 'Research on leadership in a cross-cultural context: Making progress, and raising new questions', *Leadership Quarterly*, 14 (6): 729–68.

Dickson, M.W., Resick, C.J. and Hanges, P.L. (2006) 'Systematic variations in organizationally-shared prototypes of effective leadership based on organizational form', *Leadership Quarterly*, 17 (5): 487–505.

Dionne, S.D., Yammarino, F.J., Howell, J.P. and Villa, J. (2005) 'Substitutes for leadership, or not', *Leadership Quarterly*, 16 (1): 169–93.

Doh, J.P. (2003) 'Can leadership be taught?: Perspectives from management educators', *Academy of Management Learning and Education* 2 (1): 54–68.

Dorfman, P.W. (2003) 'International and Cross-Cultural Leadership Research', in B.J. Punnett and O. Shenkar (eds) *Handbook for International Management Research*, Ann Arbor, MI: University of Michigan.

Drath, W. (2001) *The Deep Blue Sea: Rethinking the Source of Leadership*. San Francisco, CA: Jossey-Bass and Center for Creative Leadership.

Drucker, P. (1955) *The Practice of Management*. New York: Harper & Row.

Dvir, T., Eden, D., Avolio, B.J. and Shamir, B. (2002) 'Impact of transformational leadership on follower development and performance: A field experiment', *Academy of Management Journal*, 45 (4): 735–44.

Eagly, A.H. (1987) *Sex Differences in Social Behaviour: A Social-Role Interaction*. Hillsdale: Erlbaum.

Eagly, A.H., Johannesen-Schmidt, M.C. and van Engen, M. (2003) 'Transformational, transactional and laissez-faire leadership styles: A meta-analysis comparing women and men', *Psychological Bulletin*, 95: 569–91.

Eagly, A.H. and Johnson, B. (1990) 'Gender and leadership: A meta-analysis', *Psychological Bulletin*, 108: 233–56.

Elkin, G., Jackson, B. and Inkson, K. (2004) *Organizational Behaviour in New Zealand*. Auckland: Prentice-Hall.

Elmes, M. and Barry, M. (1999) 'Deliverance, denial, and the death zone: A study of narcissism and regression in the May 1996 Everest climbing disaster', *Journal of Applied Behavioral Science*, 35: 163–87.

Fiedler, F.E. (1967) *A Theory of Leadership Development*. New York: McGraw-Hill.

Fletcher, J.K. and Käufer, K. (2003) 'Shared leadership: Paradox and possibility', in C.L. Pearce and J.A. Conger (eds), *Shared Leadership: Reframing the Hows and Whys of Leadership*. Thousand Oaks, CA: Sage Publications, pp. 21–47.

Freud, S. (1921) Group psychology and the analysis of the ego', in J. Strachley (ed.), *The Standard Edition of the Complete Works of Sigmund Freud: Vol 28. Beyond the Pleasure Principle, Group Psychology and Other Works*. London: Hogarth Press, pp. 65–143.

Fry, L.W. (2003) 'Toward a theory of spiritual leadership'. *Leadership Quarterly*, 14 (6): 693–727.

Fry, L.W. (2006) 'Toward a paradigm of spiritual leadership', *Leadership Quarterly*, 16 (5): 619–22.

Fullan, M. (2001) *Leading in a Culture of Change*. San Francisco, CA: Jossey-Bass.

Gardiner, M. and Tiggemann, M. (1999) 'Gender differences in leadership style, job stress and mental health in male and female-dominated industries', *Journal of Occupational and Organizational Psychology*, 72: 301–15.

Gardner, H. (1995) *Leading Minds*. New York: Basic Books.

Gardner, W.L., and Avolio, B.J. (1998) 'The charismatic relationship: A dramaturgical perspective', *Academy of Management Review*, 23: 32–58.

Gardner, W.L., Avolio, B.J., Luthans, F., May, D.R. and Walumbwa, F. (2005) 'Can you see the real me? A self-based model of authentic leader and follower development', *Leadership Quarterly*, 16 (3): 343–72.

Goethals, G.R. (2005) 'The Psychodynamics of Leadership: Freud's Insights and Their Vicissitudes', in D.M. Messick and R.M. Kramer (eds), *The Psychology of Leadership*. Mahwah, NJ: Lawrence Erlbaum Associates, pp. 97–112.

Goffman, E. (1959) *The Presentation of Self in Everyday Life*. New York: Doubleday Anchor.

Goleman, D. (1995) *Emotional Intelligence: Why it Can Matter More than IQ*. New York: Bantam.

Goleman, D. (1998) 'What makes a leader?', *Harvard Business Review*, 76: 92–102.

Gooderham, P. and Nordhaug, O. (2001) 'Are cultural differences in Europe on the decline?', *European Business Forum*, Winter.

Gordon, J. (1992) 'Work teams: How far have they come?', *Training* (Oct): 59–65.

Gordon, R. (2002) 'Viewing the dispersion of leadership through a power lens: Exposing unobtrusive tensions and problematic processes', in K.W. Parry and J. Meindl (eds), *Grounding Leadership Theory and Research: Issues, Perspectives, and Methods*. Greenwich, CT. Information Age Publishing. pp. 39–56.

Graen, G.B. and Hui, C. (1999) 'Transcultural global leadership in the twenty-first century: Challenges and implications for development', in W.H. Mobley (ed.), *Advances in Global Leadership, Volume 1*. Stamford, CT: JAI Press, pp. 9–26.

Graen, G.B. and Uhl-Bien, M. (1995) 'Relationship-based approach to leadership: Development of leader-member-exchange (LMX) theory over 25 years: Applying a multi-level multi-domain perspective', *Leadership Quarterly*, 6: 219–47.

Greenleaf, R.K. (1977) *Servant Leadership: A Journey into the Nature of Legitimate Power and Greatness*. New York: Paulist Press.

Grey, C. (2005) *A Very Short, Fairly Interesting and Reasonably Cheap Book about Studying Organizations*. London: Sage.

Grint, K. (2001) *The Arts of Leadership*. Oxford: Oxford University Press.

Grint, K. (2005) *Leadership: Limits and Possibilities*. New York: Palgrave Macmillan.

Grint, K. (2007) Learning to lead: Can Aristotle help us to find the road to wisdom. Unpublished paper.

Gronn, P. (2002) 'Distributed leadership as a unit of analysis', *Leadership Quarterly* 13 (4): 423–51.

Gustafson, S.B. and Ritzer, D.R. (1995) 'The dark side of normal: A psychopathy-linked pattern called aberrant self-promotion', *European Journal of Personality,* 9: 147–83.

Guthey, E. (2005) 'Management studies, cultural criticism and American dreams', *Journal of Management Studies*, 42 (2): 451–66.

Guthey, E. and Jackson, B. (2005) 'CEO portraits and the authenticity paradox', *Journal of Management Studies*, 42 (5): 1057–82.

Hall, E.T. and Hall, M.R. (1990) *Understanding Cultural Differences*. Yarmouth, ME: Intercultural Press.

Hambrick, D., and Mason, P. (1984) 'Upper echelons: The organization as a reflection of its top managers', *Academy of Management Review*, 9: 193–206.

Hanges, P.J. and Dickson, M.W. (2006) 'Agitation over aggregation: Clarifying the development of and the nature of the GLOE scales', *Leadership Quarterly*, 17 (5): 522–36.

Harzing, A. (2006). 'Response styles in cross-national survey research: a 26-country study', *International Journal of Cross Cultural Management*, 6 (2): 123–41.

Heenan, D.A. and Bennis, W. (1999) *Co-leaders: The Power of Great Partnerships*. New York: John Wiley & Sons.

Henry, E., and Pene H. (2001) 'Kaupapa Maori: Locating indigenous ontology, epistemology and methodology in the academy', *Organization* 8 (2): 234–42.

Hersey, P. and Blanchard, K. (1977) *The Management of Organizational Behaviour*. Englewood Cliffs, NJ: Prentice-Hall.

Hicks, D.A. (2002) 'Spiritual and religious diversity at the workplace: Implications for leadership', *Leadership Quarterly,* 13: 379–96.

Hickson, D.J. and Pugh, D.S. (2001) *Management Worldwide: Distinctive Styles Amid Globalization*. London: Penguin.

Hofstede, G. (1980) *Culture's Consequences: International Differences in Work-Related Values*. Beverly Hills, CA: Sage.

Hofstede, G. (1991) *Cultures and Organizations: The Software of the Mind*. NewYork: McGraw-Hill.

Hofstede, G. and Bond, M.H. (1988) 'The Confucius Connection: From cultural roots to economic growth', *Organizational Dynamics*, 16 (4): 4–21.

Hogg, M.A. (2005) 'Social Identity and Leadership', in D.M. Messick, and R.M. Kramer (eds), *The Psychology of Leadership*. Hillsdale, New Jersey: Lawrence Erlbaum Associates, pp. 53–80.

Hogg, M.A., Fielding, K.S., Johnston, D., Masser, B., Russell, E. and Svensson, A. (2001) On glass ceilings and demographic disadvantage: Social identity and leadership in small groups. Unpublished manuscript, University of Queensland Centre for Research on Group Processes.

Hollander, E.P. (1958) 'Conformity, status, and idiosyncratic credit', *Psychology Review*, 65: 117–27.

Holmes, J. and Marra, M. (2004) 'Relational practice in the work place: Women's talk or gendered discourse?', *Language in Society*, 33: 377–98.

Hooker, (2003) *Working Across Cultures*. Stanford, CA: Stanford University Press.

Hosking, D.M. (1988) 'Organizing, leadership and skilful process', *Journal of Management Studies*, 25: 147–66.

Hosking, D.M. (1991) 'Chief executives, organising processes, and skill', *European Journal of Applied Psychology*, 41: 95–103.

Hosking, D. (2007) 'Not leaders, not followers: A post-modern discourse of leadership processes', in B. Shamir, R. Pillai, M. Bligh and M. Uhl-Bien (eds), *Follower-Centered Perspectives of Leadership: A Tribute to the Memory of James R. Meindl*. Greenwich, CT: Information Age Publishing, pp. 167–86.

House, R.J. (1971) A path-goal theory of leader effectiveness', *Administrative Science Quarterly*, 16: 321–39.

House, R.J. (1977) 'A 1976 theory of charismatic leadership', in J.G. Hunt and L.L Larson (eds), *Leadership: The Cutting Edge*. Carbondale, IL: Southern Illinois University Press, pp. 189–207.

House, R.J., Hanges, P., Javidan, M., Dorfman, P. and Gupta, V. (eds) (2004) *Culture, Leadership and Organisations: The GLOBE Study of 62 Societies*. Thousand Oaks, CA: Sage.

Huczynski, A. and Buchanan, D. (2006) *Organizational Behaviour*. New York: Prentice-Hall.

Hummel, R.P. (1975) 'Psychology of charismatic followers', *Psychological Reports*, 37: 759–70.

Huxham, C. and Vangen, S. (2000) 'Leadership in the shaping and implementation of collaboration agendas: How things happen in a (not quite) joined up world', *Academy of Management Journal*, 43 (6): 1159–75.

Jackall, R. (1988) *Moral Mazes*. Oxford: Oxford University Press.

Jackson, B. (2001) *Management Gurus and Management Fashions: A Dramatistic Inquiry*. London: Routledge.

Jackson, B. and Parry, K.W. (2001) *The Hero Manager: Learning from New Zealand's Top Chief Executives*. Auckland: Penguin.

Jackson, B., Pfeifer, D. and Vine, B. (2006) The co-leadership of transformational leadership: Proceedings of the Annual Meeting of the Australian and New Zealand Academy of Management, 97–114.

Jones, A.M. (2005) 'The anthropology of leadership: Culture and corporate leadership in the American South', *Leadership*, 9 (1): 259–78.

Jones, A.M. (2006) 'Developing what? An anthropological look at the leadership development process across cultures', *Leadership*, 11 (2): 481–98.

Judge, T.A., Bono, J.E., Ilies, R. and Gerhardt, M.W. (2002) 'Personality and leadership: A qualitative and quantitative review', *Journal of Applied Psychology*, 87 (4): 765–80.

Kanter, R.M. (1977) *Men and Women of the Corporation*. New York: Basic Books.

Kanter, R.M. and Corn, R.I. (1994) 'Do cultural differences make a business difference? Contextual factors affecting cross-cultural relationship success', *Journal of Management Development*, 13 (2): 5–23.

Keller, T. (2003) 'Parental images as a guide to leadership sensemaking: an attachment perspective on implicit leadership theories', *Leadership Quarterly*, 14 (2): 141–60.

Kellerman, B. and Webster, S.W. (2001) 'The recent literature on public leadership: reviewed and considered', *Leadership Quarterly*, 12 (4): 485–514.

Kelloway, E.K., Barling, J. and Helleur, J. (2000) 'Enhancing transformational leadership: the roles of training and feedback', *The Leadership and Organizational Development Journal*, 21 (3): 145–9.

Kempster, S. (2006) 'Leadership learning through lived experience', *Journal of Management & Organization*, 12 (1): 4–22.

Kerr, S. and Jermier, J. (1978) 'Substitutes for leadership: Their meaning and measurement', *Organizational Behavior and Human Performance*, 22: 374–403.

Kets de Vries, M. (2004) 'Putting leaders on the couch', *Harvard Business Review*, January.

Kets de Vries, M. (2006) *The Leader on the Couch*. Chichester, West Sussex: Jossey-Bass.

Kets de Vries, M.F.R. and Engellau, E. (2004) *Are Leaders Born or Are they Made?* London: Karnac.

Kets de Vries, M.F.R. and Miller, D. (1985) 'Narcissism and leadership: an object relations perspective', *Human Relations*, 38 (6): 583–601.

Kluckhohn, F. and Strodtbeck, F.L. (1961) *Variations in Value Orientations*. Westport, CT: Greenwood.

Knights, D. and Willmott, H. (1992) 'Conceptualizing leadership processes: a study of senior managers in a financial services company', *Journal of Management Studies*, 29: 761–82.

Kotter, J.P. (1990) *A Force for Change: How Leadership Differs from Management*. New York: Free Press.

Kouzes, J.M. and Posner, B.Z. (1998) *Encouraging the Heart*. San Francisco, CA: Jossey-Bass.

Krakauer, J. (1997) *Into Thin Air: A Personal Account of the Mount Everest Disaster*. New York: Anchor Books.

Kunda, G. (1992) *Engineering Culture: Control and Commitment in a High-Tech corporation*. Philadelphia, PA: Temple University Press.

Link, W., Corral, T. and Gerzon, M. (2006) *Leadership is Global*. Shinnyo-en Foundation.

Lipman-Blumen, J. (2007) 'Toxic leaders and the fundamental vulnerability of being alive', in B. Shamir, R. Pillai, M.C. Bligh and M. Uhl-Bien (eds), *Follower-Centered Perspectives on Leadership*, Greenwich, CT: Information Age Publishing, pp. 1–17.

Locke, E.A. (2003) 'Leadership: Starting at the top' in C.L. Pearce and J.A. Conger (eds), *Shared Leadership: Reframing the Hows and Whys of Leadership*. Thousand Oaks, CA: Sage Publications, pp. 271–84.

Lord, R.G. (1985) 'An information processing approach to social perceptions, leadership perceptions and behavioural measurement of organizational settings', in B.M. Staw and L. Cummings (eds), *Research in Organizational Behaviour,* Greenwich, CT: JAI, pp. 87–108.

Lord, R.G. and Mayer, K.G. (1991) *Leadership and Information Processing: Linking Perceptions and Performances.* Boston: Unwin Hyman.

Lynham, S.A. (2000) 'Leadership Development: A review of the theory and literature; in P. Kuchinke (ed.), *Proceedings of the 2000 Academy of Human Resource Development Annual Meeting,* Baton Rouge, LA: Academy of Human Resource Development.

Maccoby, M. (2000) 'Narcissistic leaders: The incredible pros, the inevitable cons', *Harvard Business Review,* 78 (1): 68–77.

Manz, C.C. and Sims, H.P. (1991) 'SuperLeadership: beyond the myth of heroic leadership', *Organizational Dynamics,* 19: 18–35.

Martin, J. (1993) *Cultures in Organizations: Three Perspectives.* New York: Oxford University Press.

Mayo, M., Meindl, J.R. and Pastor J.C. (2003) 'Shared leadership in work teams', in C.L. Pearce and J.A Conger (eds), *Shared Leadership: Reframing the Hows and Whys of Leadership.* Thousand Oaks, CA: Sage, pp. 193–214.

McCall, M. and Lombardo, M.M. (1988) *The Lessons of Experience.* Lexington, MA: Lexington Books.

Mead, R. (1994) *International Management: Cross-Cultural Dimensions.* Oxford: Blackwell.

Meek, V.L. (1988) 'Organizational culture: Origins and weaknesses', *Organization Studies,* 9: 453–73.

Meindl, J.R. (1993) 'Reinventing leadership: A radical social psychological approach', in J.D. Murningham (ed.), *Social Psychology in Organizations.* Englewood Clifffs, NJ: Prentice-Hall, pp. 89–118.

Meindl, J. (1995) 'The romance of leadership as a follower-centric theory: A social constructionist approach', *Leadership Quarterly,* 6 (3): 329–41.

Meindl, J.R., Ehrlich, S.B. and Dukerich, J.M. (1985) 'The romance of leadership', *Administrative Science Quarterly,* 30 (1): 78–102.

Meindl, J.R. and Ehrlich, S.B. (1987) 'The romance of leadership and the evaluation of organizational performance', *Academy of Management Journal,* 30 (1): 91–109.

Meindl, J.R. and Ehrlich, S.B. (1988) 'Developing a "romance of leadership" scale', *Proceedings of the Eastern Academy of Management,* pp. 133–5.

Meindl, J.R., Pastor, J.C. and Mayo, M. (2004) 'Romance of leadership', in G.R Goethals, G.J. Sorenson and J.M. Burns (eds) *Encyclopedia of Leadership* (Vol. 3). Thousand Oaks, CA: Sage Publications, pp. 233–45.

Michalko, M. (2001) *Cracking Creativity: The Secrets of Creative Genius for Business and Beyond*. Berkeley, CA: Ten Speed Press.

Messick, D.M. (2005) 'On the psychological exchange between leaders and followers', in D.M. Messick and R.M. Kramer (eds), *The Psychology of Leadership*. Hillsdale, NJ: Lawrence Erlbaum Associates, pp. 81–96.

Mobley, W.H. and Weldon, E. (2006) *Advances in Global Leadership (Volume 4)*. New York: Elsevier JAI.

Mumford, M.D. and Van Doorn, J. (2001) 'The leadership of pragmatism: reconsidering Franklin in the age of charisma', *Leadership Quarterly*, 12: 279–310.

Neale, J. (2001) 'Against the odds: Combining family and the leadership role', in K.W. Parry (ed.), *Leadership in the Antipodes: Findings, Implications and a Leader Profile*. Wellington, NZ: Institute of Policy Studies and the Centre for the Study of Leadership, pp. 141–65.

Nielsen, J. (2004) *The Myth of Leadership: Creating Leaderless Organizations*. Palo Alto, CA: Davies-Black.

O'Toole, J., Galbraith, J. and Lawler, E.E. (2003) 'The promise and pitfalls of shared leadership', in C.L. Pearce and J.A. Conger (eds) *Shared Leadership: Reframing the Hows and Whys of Leadership*. Thousand Oaks, CA: Sage Publications, pp. 250–67.

Offerman, L.R. (2004) 'When followers become toxic', *Harvard Business Review*, January, 55–60.

Osborn, R.N., Hunt, J.G. and Jauch, L.R. (2002) 'Toward a contextual theory of leadership', *Leadership Quarterly*, 13 (6): 797–837.

Osland, J.S., Bird, A., Delano, J. and Jacob, M. (2000) 'Beyond sophisticated stereotyping: Cultural sensemaking in context', *Academy of Management Executive*, 14 (1): 65–79.

Oswick, C., Keenoy, T. and Grant, D. (2002) 'Metaphors and analogical reasoning in organization theory: beyond orthodoxy', *Academy of Management Review*, 27 (2): 294–303.

Ottensmeyer, E. (1996) 'Too strong to stop, too sweet to lose: Aesthetics as a way to know organizations', *Organization*, 3 (2): 189–94.

Palmer, I. and Hardy, C. (2001) *Thinking About Management*. Thousand Oaks, CA: Sage Publications.

Parry, K.W. (1999) 'Enhancing adaptability: leadership strategies to accommodate change in local government settings', *Journal of Organizational Change Management*, 12 (2): 134–56.

Parry, K.W. (2004) *Becoming a Transformational Leader*. Brisbane: Management Press.

Parry, K.W. and Bryman, A. (2006) 'Leadership in Organizations', in S. Clegg, C. Hardy and W. Nord (eds), *Handbook of Organization Studies* (2nd edn). London: Sage, pp. 447–68.

Parry, K.W. and Proctor-Thomson, S.B. (2002) 'Perceived integrity of transformational leaders in organizational settings', *Journal of Business Ethics*, 35 (2): 75–96.

Parry, K.W. and Proctor-Thomson, S.B. (2003) 'Leadership, culture and performance: The case of the New Zealand public sector', *Journal of Change Management*, 3 (4): 376–99.

Parry, K.W. and Sinha, P. (2005) 'Researching the Trainability of Transformational Organizational Leadership', *Human Resource Development International*, 8 (2): 165–83.

Parsons, T. and Shils, E.A. (1951) *Towards a General Theory of Action*. Cambridge, MA: Harvard University Press.

Pearce, C.L. and Conger, J.A. (eds) (2003). *Shared Leadership: Reframing the Hows and Whys of Leadership*. Thousand Oaks, CA: Sage Publications.

Pearce, C.L. and Sims, H.P. (2000) 'Shared leadership: Toward a multi-level theory of leadership', *Advances in the Interdisciplinary Studies of Work Teams*, 7: 115–39.

Pearson, C.A.L. (1992) 'Autonomous work-groups: An evaluation at an industrial site', *Human Relations*, 45: 905–36.

Peters, T. and Austin, N. (1985) *A Passion for Excellence: The Leadership Difference*. New York: HarperCollins.

Peterson, M.F. and Castro, S.L. (2006) 'Measurement metrics at aggregate levels of analysis: Implications of organization culture research and the GLOBE project', *Leadership Quarterly*, 17 (5): 506–21.

Pfeffer, J. (1977) 'The ambiguity of leadership', *Academy of Management Review*, 2: 104–12.

Pfeffer, J. and Salancik, G.R. (1978) *The External Control of Organizations: A Resource Dependency Perspective*. New York: Harper & Row.

Pfeifer, D., Love, M. and Jackson, B. (2006) 'Exploring intra-national cross-cultural leadership: The case of New Zealand Aotearoa. Paper presented at the Academy of Management Meeting, Atlanta, GA.

Podsakoff, P.M., MacKenzie, S.B., Moorman, R.H. and Fetter, R. (1990) 'Transformational leader behaviours and their effects on followers' trust in leader, satisfaction, and organizational citizenship behaviors', *Leadership Quarterly*, 1: 107–42.

Popper, M. (2001) *Hypnotic Leadership: Leaders, Followers, and the Loss of Self*. Westport, CT: Praeger.

Post, J.M. (1986) 'Narcissism and the charismatic leader-follower relationship'. *Political Psychology*, 7 (4): 675–87.

Porter, L.W. and McLaughlin, G.B. (2006) 'Leadership and the organizational context: Like the weather?', *Leadership Quarterly*, 17 (6): 559–76.

Prince, L. (2005) 'Eating the menu rather than the dinner: Tao and leadership', *Leadership*, 1 (1): 105–26.

Pye, A. (2005) 'Leadership and organizing: Sense-making in action', *Leadership*, 1 (1): 31–50.

Raelin, J. (2003) *Creating Leaderful Organisations: How to Bring Out Leadership in Everyone*. San Francisco, CA: Berrett-Koehler.

Ropo, A. and Eriksson, M. (1997) 'Managing a theatre production: Conflict, communication, and competence', in M. Fitzgibbon and A. Kelly (eds), *From Maestro to Manager: Critical Issues in Arts and Culture Management*. Dublin: Oak Tree Press.

Ropo, A., Parviainen, J. and Koivunen, N. (2002) 'Aesthetics in leadership: From absent bodies to social bodily presence', in K.W. Parry and J.R. Meindl (eds), *Grounding Leadership Theory and Research: Issues, Perspectives and Methods*. Greenwich, CT: Information Age Publishing, pp. 21–38.

Rosener, J.B. (1997) 'Sexual static', in K. Grint (ed.), *Leadership: Classical, Contemporary and Critical Approaches*. Oxford: Oxford University Press, pp. 211–33.

Rost, J.C. (1993) *Leadership for the Twenty-First Century*. Westport, CT: Praeger.

Sally, D. (2002) 'Co-leadership: Lessons from republican Rome', *California Management Review*, 44: 65–83.

Sass, J.S. (2000) 'Characterizing organizational spirituality: An organizational communication culture approach', *Communication Studies*, 51: 195–207.

Schein, E.H. (2004) *Organizational Culture and Leadership* (3rd edn). San Francisco, CA: Jossey-Bass.

Schwartz, S.H. (1999) 'Cultural value differences: Some implications for work', *Applied Psychology: An International Review*, 48: 23–48.

Schyns, B. and Meindl, J.R. (2005) *Implicit Leadership Theories*. Greenwich, CT: Information Age Publishing.

Shackleton, E. (1999) *South: The Endurance Expedition*. New York: Signet.

Shamir, B. (1992) 'Attribution of influence and charisma to the leader: The romance of leadership revisited'. *Journal of Applied Social Psychology*, 22: 386–407.

Shamir, B., House, R.J. and Arthur, M.B. (1993) 'The motivational effects of charismatic leadership: A self-concept based theory', *Organisation Science*, 4 (4): 577–94.

Shamir, B. and Howell, J.M. (1999) 'Organizational and contextual influences on the emergence and effectiveness of charismatic leadership', *Leadership Quarterly*, 10 (2): 257–83.

Shamir, B. and Lapidot, Y. (2003) 'Shared leadership in the management of group boundaries', in C.L. Pearce and J.A. Conger (eds), *Shared Leadership: Reframing the Hows and Whys of Leadership*. Thousand Oaks, CA: Sage, pp. 235–49.

Shamir, B. (2007) 'From Passive Recipients to Active Co-Producers', in B. Shamir, R. Pillai, M.C. Bligh and M. Uhl-Bien (eds), *Follower-centered Perspectives on Leadership,* Greenwich, CT: Information Age Publishing, pp. ix–xxxix.

Shane, S., Venkataraman, V. and MacMillan, I. (1995) 'Cultural differences in innovation championing roles', *Journal of Management,* 26: 931–52.

Shaw, J.B. (1990) 'A cognitive categorization model for the study of intercultural management', *Academy of Management Review,* 15: 626–45.

Sims, H.P. and Lorenzi, P. (1992) *The New Leadership Paradigm.* Newbury Park, CA: Sage.

Sinclair, A. (2005) 'Body possibilities in leadership', *Leadership,* 1 (4): 387–406.

Sinclair, A. (2007) *Leadership for the Disillusioned.* Crows Nest, NSW: Allen & Unwin.

Smircich, L. (1993) 'Concepts of culture and organizational analysis', *Administrative Science Quarterly,* 28: 339–58.

Smircich, L. and Morgan, G. (1982) 'Leadership: the management of meaning', *Journal of Applied Behavioural Science,* 18: 257–73.

Smith, M.A. and Canger, J.M. (2004) 'Effects of superior 'big five' personality on subordinates attitudes', *Journal of Business and Psychology,* 18 (4): 465–81.

Søderberg, A-M and Holden, N. (2002) 'Rethinking Cross Cultural Management in a Globalizing Business World', *International Journal of Cross Cultural Management,* 2 (1): 103–21.

Sonnenfeld, J.A. and Ward, A. (2007) *Firing Back: How Great Leaders Rebound after Career Setbacks.* Cambridge, MA: HBS Press.

Sosik, J., Avolio, B. and Kahai, S. (1997). Effects of leadership style and anonymity on group potency and effectiveness in a group decision support system environment. *Journal of Applied Psychology,* 82 (1): 89–103.

Stafsudd, A. (2004) 'People are strange when you're a stranger: Senior executives select similar successors', *European Management Review,* 3: 177–89.

Starratt, R.J. (1993) *The Drama of Leadership.* London: Falmer Press.

Stech, E.L. (2004) 'Psychodynamic approach', in Northouse, P.G. (ed.), *Leadership Theory and Practice.* London: Sage, pp. 235–63.

Stogdill, R.M. (1974) *Handbook of Leadership.* New York: Free Press.

Storey, J. (2004) 'Changing theories of leadership and leadership development', in J. Storey (ed), *Leadership in Organizations: Current Issues and Key Trends.* London: Routledge, pp. 11–37.

Tayeb, M.H. (1996) 'Conducting research across cultures: Overcoming drawbacks and obstacles', *International Journal of Cross-Cultural Management,* 1 (9): 91–108.

Thomas, D. and Inkson, K. (2004) *Cultural Intelligence: People Skills for Global Business*. San Francisco, CA: Berrett-Koehler.

Ting-Tommey, S. (1988) 'Intercultural conflict styles', in Y. Kim and W. Gudykunst (eds), *Theories in Intercultural Communication*. Thousand Oaks, CA: Sage.

Triandis, H. (1980) *Handbook of Cross-cultural Psychology*. Boston, MA: Allyn & Bacon.

Trompenaars, F. and Hampden-Turner, C. (1997) *Riding the Waves of Culture: Understanding Cultural Diversity in Business*. London: Nicholas Brealey.

Turner, V. (1974) *Dramas, Fields, and Metaphors*. Ithaca and London: Cornell University Press.

Uhl-Bien, M. and Pillai, R. (2007) 'The romance of leadership and the social construction of *followership*', in B. Shamir, R. Pillai, M.C. Bligh, and M. Uhl-Bien (eds), *Follower-centred Perspectives on Leadership*. Greenwich, CT: IAP publishing, pp. 187–209.

Van Knippenberg, D. and Hogg, M.A. (2003) 'A social identity model of leadership effectiveness in organizations', in B.M. Staw and R.M. Kramer (eds), *Research in Organizational Behaviour* (Vol. 25). New York: Elsevier, pp. 243–95.

Vroom, V.H. and Yetton, P.W. (1973) *Leadership and Decision-making*. Pittsburgh, PA: University of Pittsburgh Press.

Waldman, D.A., Bass, B.M. and Yammarino, F.J. (1990) 'Adding to contingent reward behaviour: The augmenting effect of charismatic leadership', *Group and Organization Studies*, 15 (4): 381–94.

Walker, H., Ilardi, B., McMahon, A. and Fennell, M. (1996) 'Gender, interaction, and leadership', *Social Psychology Quarterly*, 59: 255–72.

Warner, L.S. and Grint, K. (2006) 'American Indian ways of leading and knowing', *Leadership*, 2 (2): 225–44.

Watson, T.J. (1994) *In Search of Management*. London: Routledge.

Weick, K.E. (1995) *Sensemaking in Organizations*. Thousand Oaks, CA: Sage.

Weick, K.E. (2007) 'Romancing, following, and sensemaking: James Meindl's legacy', in B. Shamir, R. Pillai, Bligh, M.C. and M. Uhl-Bien (eds), *Follower-centred Perspectives on Leadership*. Greenwich, CT: IAP publishing, pp. 279–91.

Yukl, G.A. (1999) 'An evaluation of conceptual weaknesses in transformational and charismatic leadership theories', *Leadership Quarterly*, 10 (2): 285–305.

Yukl, G.A. (2002) *Leadership in Organizations*. Upper Saddle River, NJ: Prentice Hall.

Zaleznik, A. (1970) 'Power and politics in organizational life', *Harvard Business Review*, 48: 47–60.

Zaleznik, A. (1977) 'Managers and leaders: are they different?', *Harvard Business Review*, 55: 67–78.

Appendix: Resources for Studying Leadership

██████ nine very useful leadership reference books

Antonakis, J., Cianciolo, A.T. and Sternberg, R.J. (2004) *The Nature of Leadership*. Thousand Oaks, CA: Sage Publications.

Avery, G.C. (2005) *Understanding Leadership: Paradigms and Cases*. London: Sage Publications.

Bass, B. (1990) *Bass & Stogdill's Handbook of Leadership: Theory, Research and Managerial Applications*. New York: Free Press.

Goethals, G.R., Sorenson, G.J. and Burns, J.M. (2004) *Encyclopedia of Leadership* (Vol. 1–4). Thousand Oaks, CA: Sage Publications.

Marturano, A. and Gosling, J. (eds.) (2007). *Leadership: The Key Concepts*. Oxford: Routledge.

Northouse, P.G. (2007) *Leadership: Theory and Practice* (4th edn.). Thousand Oaks, CA: Sage Publications.

Storey, J. (ed.) (2004) *Leadership in Organizations: Current Issues and Key Trends*. London: Routledge.

Wren, T. Hicks, D. and Price, T. (eds) (2004). *The International Library of Leadership*. Cheltenham: Edward Elgar.

Yukl, G.A. (2006) *Leadership in Organizations* (6th edn.). Upper Saddle River, NJ: Prentice Hall.

██████ ten leadership books you should read
before you die

Bass, B.M. and Avolio, B.J. (eds) (1994) *Improving Organizational Effectiveness through Transformational Leadership*. Thousand Oaks, CA: Sage Publications.

Burns, J.M. (1978) *Leadership*. New York: Harper & Row.

Greenleaf, R.K. and Spears, L. C. (2002) *Servant Leadership: A Journey into the Nature of Legitimate Power and Greatness* (25th anniversary edn.). New York: Paulist Press.

Gardner, J.W. (1990) *On Leadership*. New York: Free Press.

Grint, G. (2005) *Leadership: Limits and Possibilities*. New York: Palgrave Macmillan.

Harter, N. (2006) *Clearings in the Forest: On the Study of Leadership*. West Lafayayette, IN: Purdue University Press.

Heifetz, R. (1994) *Leadership without Easy Answers*. Cambridge, MA: Harvard University Press.

Kouzes, J.M., and Posner, B.Z. (2002) *Leadership Challenge* (3rd edn.). San Francisco, CA: Jossey-Bass.

Pearce, C.L. and Conger, J.A. (eds.) (2003) *Shared Leadership: Reframing the Hows and Whys of Leadership*. Thousand Oaks, CA: Sage Publications.

Sinclair, A. (2007) *Leadership for the Disillusioned*. Crows Nest, NSW: Allen & Unwin.

And of course....

Jackson, B. and Parry, K. (2007) *A Very Short, Fairly Interesting and Reasonably Cheap Book About Studying Leadership*. London: Sage.

seven leadership journals worth monitoring

International Journal of Leadership Studies
Journal of Leadership and Organizational Studies
Journal of Management & Organization
Journal of Organisational Behaviour
Leadership
The Leadership Quarterly
Leadership and Organization Development Journal

four associations with a leadership focus

Academy of Management (AOM)
http://www.aomonline.org/

Network of Leadership Scholars List Serve:
LDRNET-L@aomlists.pace.edu

International Leadership Association (ILA)
http://www.ila-net.org/

Social Science Research Network (SSRN)
http://www.ssrn.com/

fifteen leadership research centres worth investigating

Banff Centre Leadership Development
http://www.banffcentre.ca/departments/leadership/

Centre for Leadership Studies (University of Exeter)
http://www.leadership-studies.com/

Center for Leadership Studies (University of Binghamton)
http://cls.binghamton.edu/

Center for Public Leadership (Harvard University)
http://www.ksg.harvard.edu/leadership/

Centre for the Study of Leadership (Victoria University of Wellington)
http://www.vuw.ac.nz/vms/disciplines/CSL/index.aspx

Fuqua/Coach K Center of Leadership and Ethics (Duke University)
http://www.leadershipandethics.org

Gallup Leadership Institute (University of Nebraska)
http://gli.unl.edu/

Institute for Leadership Research (Texas Tech University)
http://www.ilr.ba.ttu.edu/

Jepson School of Leadership Studies (University of Richmond)
http://www.jepson.richmond.edu

Leader to Leader Institute (Drucker Foundation for Nonprofit Management)
http://www.leadertoleader.org/

Excelerator: New Zealand Leadership Institute (University of Auckland)
http://www.excelerator.co.nz/page/excelerator_5.php

School of Global Leadership & Entrepreneurship (Regent University)
http://www.regent.edu/acad/global/home

The Lancaster Leadership Centre (Lancaster University)
http://www.lums.lancs.ac.uk/leadership/

The James MacGregor Burns Academy of Leadership (University of Maryland)
http://www.academy.umd.edu/

Wharton Center for Leadership and Change Management (University of Pennsylvania)
http://leadership.wharton.upenn.edu/welcome/index.shtml

twenty-two movies about leadership really worth viewing

Bridge on the River Kwai (1957) Director: David Lean
Cry Freedom (1987) Director: Richard Attenborough

Dead Poet's Society (1989) Director: Peter Weir
Downfall (Der Untergang) (2004) Director: Oliver Hirschbiegel
Gandhi (1982) Director: Richard Attenborough
Glory (1989) Director: Edward Zwick
Hoosiers (1986) Director: David Anspaugh
Hotel Rwanda (2004) Director: Terry George
Kagemusha (1980) Director: Akira Kurosawa
The Last King of Scotland (2006) Director: Kevin Macdonald
Lawrence of Arabia (1962) Director: David Lean
Malcolm X (1992) Director: Spike Lee
Michael Collins (1996) Director: Neil Jordan
Norma Rae (1970) Director: Martin Ritt
Saint Joan (1957) Director: Otto Preminger
Silkwood (1983) Director: Mike Nichols
Spartacus (1960) Director: Stanley Kubrick
The Election (Hong Kong) (2005) Director: Johnny To
Thirteen Days (2000) Director: Roger Donaldson
Twelve Angry Men (1957) Director: Sidney Lumet
Wall Street (1987) Director: Oliver Stone
Whale Rider (2002) Director: Niki Caro

Index

Academy of Management (AOM) 12, 100
achievement orientation 18, 71
action learning 117
Advances in Global Leadership (Mobley and Weldon) 68
aesthetics and leadership *see* art of leadership
affiliation, need for 18
  see also relationship-oriented behaviour; task-oriented behaviour
Ailon-Souday, G. 80
Airstream company 38
Alban-Metcalfe, R.J. 30, 31, 32
Alimo-Metcalfe, B. 30, 31, 32
Alvarez, J.L. 84, 87
Alvesson, M. 56, 63, 109–10
'anthropology of leadership' 79, 122–3
anti-narcissistic leaders 37–9
art of leadership
  and bodily knowledge 109–10
  importance 104
  and interdisciplinary nature of leadership 11
  leadership as drama 110–11
  metaphors 104–6
  and sense-making 106–8
Arts of Leadership, The (Grint) 59, 104
ascription-oriented societies 71
aspiration 18, 121
assertiveness 72
assignments, developmental 116–17
associations, leadership 12, 148

Astin, H.S. 26
'attribution errors' 75
Austin, N. 13
authentic leadership 39, 98–100
autobiographies 5
Aviator, The 110
avoidance, of managers 45–6
avoidance, of uncertainty as societal cultural dimension 72, 74
Avolio, B.J. 16–17, 23, 25, 29–30, 84, 85, 88, 91, 94, 107, 111
Awamleh, R. 47

Babiak, P. 36
Badaracco, J.L. 38
Barker, J.R. 93
Barnard, C. 109
Barry, M. 37
Bass, B.M. 12, 25, 29, 30, 31, 32, 34, 85, 88, 97, 98, 100
Bathurst, Ralph 11
behaviour, leader see leader behaviour
Bennis, W.G. 18, 83, 85–6, 87
Berson, Y. 84
Bird, A. 74–5
Blair, Tony 33, 59
Blanchard, K. 44
boards of directors 95
bodily knowledge 109–10
Boje, D.M. 94–5, 108
Bond, M.H. 73
books 4, 20, 42, 67, 128, 147–8
Bratton, J. 59
Brenner, Rick 107

Brown, M.E. 91
Bryman, A. 88, 90, 102
Buffet, Warren 38
bureaucratic control 93, 120
  see also hierarchies
Burns, J.M. 11–12, 15, 85
Burr, Donald 48

Calás, M.B. 104
Cammock, P. 109
captaincy, metaphor of
  leadership 105–6
careers 114
case studies 31, 37, 92–3, 102–3
causal influences, authentic and
  inauthentic leadership
  99–100
celebrity 49
Centre for the Study of
  Leadership 6, 87, 149
centres and institutes, leadership
  6, 10, 87, 114, 148–9
CEOs 39, 55, 86, 87
CFOs 55, 86
Chairmen 55, 86
challenges, and developing
  leadership 116, 117
change 78–9
charismatic leadership 33–4, 44,
  47, 76, 111
  see also post-charismatic
  leadership
Chen, C.C. 48
child-parent relationship 50–1,
  58–9, 98
childhood experiences 16–17,
  50, 115
*Co-leaders: the Power of Great
  Partnerships* (Heenan and
  Bennis) 83
co-leadership 55, 83–4, 85–8, 120
co-producers of leadership
  14–15, 57–60, 88, 121–2

coaching, executive 117
collectivism 70–1, 74
Collins, J. 37–8, 90
Collinson, D. 59–60
communication skills 118
communication styles 84
concertive control 93
conferences 12, 69
confidence 17
Confucian dynamism 73
Conger, J.A. 34, 115
connection 17
construction of leadership
  general model, development
    of 54–5
  psychoanalytic theories 49–52
  romance of leadership theory
    47–9
  social identity theory 52–4
context 61–2, 69, 84
  see also organizational
    contexts; situational
    leadership; situational
    validity; work environment
contingency theory 45
control
  and information technology 91
  and organizational culture 65
  and self-managed work teams
    92, 93, 94
  as societal cultural dimension
    73–4, 81
  and transactional leadership
    102–3
  see also empowerment; power
Corn, R.I. 75
corporate scandals 38–9, 102
Craig, S.B. 35
*Creating Leaderful
  Organizations* (Raelin) 56
creativity 15
critical management
  studies 100

critical perspectives on leadership
  co-leadership 55, 83–4, 85–7
  developing leadership 123
  distributed leadership 88–92,
      95–6
  leaderless work groups 92–4
  shared transformational
      leadership 85–8
  team leadership 94–5
critical realism 99–100
cross-cultural leadership 67–8
cult leaders 51
cultural intelligence 67–8
'cultural paradoxes' 74
cultural perspectives on leadership
  caveats to research studies
      78–9
  critiques of research studies
      68–70, 74–5, 77–8
  cross-cultural leadership 67–8
  cultural influences on studying
      leadership 68–70
  culture, concept of 63–4
  follower perceptions and
      GLOBE study 75–8
  humanities-based perspective
      79–81, 122–3
  organizational culture 62,
      64–7, 120
  societal cultural dimensions
      70–5, 80
culture, defined 63–4
culture shock 67
Culture Shock! series 67

dark side, of leadership 36, 102
Day, D.V. 122
deconstruction 54
  see also failure, leaders
Den Hartog, D.N. 31, 69, 70,
      76, 77
developing leadership
  formal training 117–19

developing leadership *cont.*
  funding 9–10, 113, 119
  for the future 120–4
  interest in 9–10
  learning and teaching
      processes 109, 115–16,
      117, 123–4
  on-the job 116–17
  problems 119–20
  versus researching
      leadership 113–14
  resources for 113, 119
development assessment centres
      116, 120
development programmes 10,
      30, 117, 122–3
Dickson, M.W. 69, 70, 77
discourse analysis 84, 108
distributed leadership 56–7,
      88–92, 120
Doh, J.P. 115
doing leadership 5–6, 109
  see also developing leadership;
      experience, and develop-
      ing leadership
domestic situation 27
  see also childhood experi-
      ences; families; parent-
      child relationship;
      parenting
Dorfman, P.W. 78–9
dot.com bubble, bursting of
      38–9
drama, leadership as 110–11
dramaturgical analysis 111
Drucker, P. 19
dyads 55, 84

e-commerce 90–1
Eagly, A.H. 25, 26
'ecological fallacy' 77
Ehrlich, S.B. 47
Elkin, G. 85

Elmes, M. 37
'emically-oriented' leadership
    research 79–81
emotional cultural dimension
    72–3
emotional intelligence 18, 121
empirical research 56, 119–20
empowerment 90, 93
    see also control; power
'enhancing adaptability' 28
Enron 102
Eriksson, M. 109
ethical leadership 12, 38, 39,
    97, 122–3
    see also authentic leadership;
        morality; spirituality of
        leadership; values
ethnography 11, 79–80, 93,
    120, 127–8
'etically-oriented' leadership
    research 79, 82
European contexts 69
Excelerator 10, 114, 149
executive coaching 117
experience, and developing
    leadership 5–6, 109,
    115–16, 123, 124
experimental studies
    119–20

failure, leaders 5–6, 53, 55, 59
families 27, 49–51
    see also childhood
        experiences; husbands;
        parent-child relationship;
        parenting; wives
feedback 58, 116
femininity 26, 72, 74
    see also gender; wives; women
        versus men as leaders
Few Good Men, A 111
Firing Back (Sonnenfeld and
    Ward) 5–6

*Follower-Centered Perspectives
    on Leadership* (Shamir
    et al., eds.) 43
followers
    and authentic leadership 98
    books 42
    and charismatic leadership 34,
        44, 47
    and co-leadership 55, 84,
        85–8
    as co-producers of leadership
        14–15, 57–60, 88, 121–2
    as constructors of leadership
        (*see* construction of
        leadership)
    development of 121–2
    and distributed leadership
        88–92, 95–6
    importance to leadership 43
    and inauthentic leadership 98
    and leaderless work groups
        92–4
    leaders as followers 41–2
    and leadership development
        121–2
    managers as followers 24
    as moderators of leadership
        44–5, 46
    and narcissistic leaders 36
    as participants in leadership
        research 127
    perceptions of leadership
        across cultures and
        GLOBE study
        75–8
    post-structuralist
        approaches 59–60
    as recipients of leadership 44
    reluctance to be 41, 42
    and shared leadership 55–7,
        83–4, 94
    and shared transformational
        leadership 85–8

followers *cont.*
  and spirituality of leadership
    100, 101
  as substitutes of leadership
    45–6
  and team leadership 94–5
  terminology 42
  and transformational
    leadership 28–9, 30, 31,
    44, 85–8, 98
formal leaders 18–19
formal training, in developing
  leadership 117–19
framing 108
Franklin, Benjamin 102–3
Freud, S. 49, 50–1
Fry, L.W. 101
Fullan, M. 102
funding 9–10, 113, 114, 119
future research areas
  authentic and inauthentic
    leadership 99–100
  choosing 124–5
  developing leadership 120
  dramaturgical studies 111
  ethnographic studies
    119, 127–8
  experimental studies
    119–20
  metaphors of leadership 104
  narcissistic leaders 37
  new leadership and
    transformational
    leadership 32–3
  personality disorders and
    leadership 36
  pragmatic leadership 103
  psychoanalytic theories 52
  questionnaire studies 120
  self-managed work teams
    92–3
  senior leaders 127
  shared leadership 120

future research areas *cont.*
  spiritual leadership 101–2
  team leadership 95, 120

Gardner, H. 3, 14
Gardner, W.L. 39, 47, 99, 111
gender 25–8, 104
  see also femininity; masculinity
Gioia, D.A. 91
global industry of leadership
  development 9, 119
global leadership 68
  see also internationalization
    of leadership
GLOBE study 76–8
Goethals, G.R. 50–1, 52
Goleman, D. 18, 121
Gordon, J. 92
Gordon, R. 90, 91, 120
Graen, G.B. 58, 68
Greenleaf, R.K. 57
Grey, C. 20
Grint, K. 13, 14, 58, 59, 80, 95,
  104, 119, 123–4
Group Support Systems 90–1
groups 52–3
Gustafson, S.B. 35, 36
Guthey, E. 38–9, 78–9

haiku poetry 107–8
Hall, E.T. 72–3
Hall, M.R. 72–3
Hampden-Turner, C. 73–4
Hardy, C. 66, 108
Harzing, A. 77–8
Heenan, D.A. 83, 85–6, 87
Henry, E. 80
hero leaders 72
Hero Manager, The (Jackson
  and Parry) 66
'hero manager backlash' 38–9
Hersey, P. 44
Hicks, D.A. 100–1

hierarchies 62, 71, 81, 93, 120
higher purpose of leadership
  art of leadership (*see* art of
    leadership)
  authentic leadership 98–100
  post-charismatic and
    post-transformational
    leadership 102–3
  spirituality of leadership 100–2
Hitler, Adolph 97–8
Hofstede, G. 63–4, 69, 70–2,
  73, 74, 76, 80
Hogg, M.A. 52–3
Hollander, E.P. 57
Hosking, D.M. 89–90, 122
House, R.J. 34, 45, 76–8
Hubbard, Dick 66
Hui, C. 68
human capital 122
human nature, assumptions
  about, as societal cultural
  dimension 73
humanities-based perspective
  79–81, 122–3
  see also discourse analysis;
    dramaturgical analysis;
    ethnography; narrative
    analysis
humour 107
husbands 25–6

IBM 70–2
identity 23–4, 52–4
implicit leadership theory 8
In Search of Management
  (Watson) 128
inauthentic leadership 98,
  99–100
individual differences 75, 77, 78
individual leadership, in team
  leadership 95
individualism 70–1, 74
industries, gender composition
  26–7

industry, global, of leadership
  development 9, 119
informal leaders 19
information technology 90–1
Inkson, K. 67–8, 85
inspirational leadership 99
institutes and centres of leadership
  6, 10, 87, 114, 148–9
integrity 17, 35
International Leadership
  Association (ILA) 12, 148
internationalization of leadership 11, 12
  see also global leadership

Jackall, R. 128
Jackson, B. 38–9, 66, 78, 83–4,
  85, 95
Jermier, J. 45
Johnson, B. 25, 26
Jones, A.M. 79, 122–3
journals 11, 39, 46, 148
Judge, T.A. 35
Jung, C. 49

Kanter, R.M. 75, 127
Kaupapa Maori research 80
Kellerman, B. 85
Kempster, S. 100
Kerr, S. 45
Kets de Vries, M.F.R. 17, 37, 51
Kluckhohn, F. 73
Knights, D. 89
knowledge 68, 123
Kotter, J.P. 18–19, 31
Kouzes, J.M. 31, 88, 89
Krakauer, J. 37
Kunda, G. 65, 80, 128

Lapidot, Y. 94
leader behaviour
  development 115, 116,
    117–18
  gender differences 26–7

leader behaviour *cont.*
  theories 24–5
  transformational leadership
    29–30, 32
  see also relationship-oriented
    behaviour; task-oriented
    behaviour
leader categories 52
leader identity 23–4, 52-4
Leader-Member-Exchange
  (LMX) theory 58
leader schemas 52
leaderless work groups 92–4
leadership
  art of (*see* art of leadership)
  critical perspectives (*see*
    critical perspectives on
    leadership)
  cultural perspectives (*see*
    cultural perspectives on
    leadership)
  definitional problems and
    ambiguities 12–15, 56,
    109–10
  demystification 3, 14
  elements 15
  higher purpose (*see* higher
    purpose of leadership)
  interdisciplinary and applied
    nature 10–12
  'level 4' 37, 39
  'level 5' 37–8, 39, 90
  versus management 18–19,
    24, 31
    see also managers
  metaphors 58–9, 104–7, 108
  nature-nurture debate 16–17,
    23, 115
  as social construction 43, 48
  substitution 45–6
  traits 17–18, 23–4, 34–6, 118
  see also developing leadership;
    researching leadership;
    studying leadership

Leadership 11
*Leadership: Limits and
  Possibilities* (Grint) 13
leadership associations 12, 148
leadership capabilities 88–9
leadership centres and institutes
  6, 10, 87, 114, 148–9
Leadership for the Disillusioned
  (Sinclair) 123
leadership programmes 10, 30,
  117, 122–3
Leadership Quarterly, The 11, 46
leadership skills 89–90, 115,
  116, 117–18, 123, 124
leadership styles, and situational
  leadership 44–5
learning processes, in developing
  leadership 109, 115–16,
  117, 123–4
Learning to Lead (Conger) 115
Leland, C. 26
'level 4 leadership' 37, 39
'level 5 leadership' 37–8,
  39, 90
Levy, L. 19
library research 128
Lind, A. 19
linguistic cultural dimension
  72–3
Lipman-Blumen, J. 51
literature searching 126, 128
locus of control 18
Lord, R.G. 52, 75
Love, M. 78

Maccoby, M. 36, 37
management, *versus* leadership
  18–19, 24, 31
'management of meaning'
  28, 62, 101
managers
  avoidance of 45–6
  and leaders 18–19, 24, 31
  and leadership skills 89, 90

managers *cont*
  and self-managed work
     teams 92
  self-promotion 36
Manufacturing Consent
  (Kunda) 128
Manz, C.C. 88
masculinity 72, 74, 104
  see also femininity; gender;
     men *versus* women as
     leaders; husbands
Mayer, K.G. 75
Mayo, M. 94
McLaughlin, G.B. 62
media 38–9, 48–9
  see also books; information
     technology; journals;
     movies; newspapers;
     writing about leadership
Meindl, J.R. 8, 43, 47, 48, 75
*Men and Women of the
  Corporation* (Kanter) 127
men *versus* women as leaders
  25–8
  see also gender; masculinity
mentoring 117
Messick, D.M. 57
metaphors 58–9, 104–7, 108
methodologies 125, 127–8
  see also case studies; discourse
     analysis; dramaturgical
     analysis; empirical
     research; ethnography;
     experimental studies;
     narrative analysis;
     qualitative methodologies;
     quantitative methodologies;
     questionnaires; validity
Michalko, M. 104
mindfulness 68
minorities, and social identity
  theory 53–4

Mobley, W.H. 68
moderation of leadership
  44–5, 46
Moral Mazes (Jackall) 128
morality 3, 12, 98–9, 100, 122–3
  see also authentic leadership;
     ethical leadership; religion;
     spirituality of leadership;
     values
Morgan, G. 28
motivations 99, 101
movies 4, 38, 59, 110, 111,
  149–50
multi-source feedback 116
multibillion-dollar global
  industry of leadership
  development 9, 119
Multifactor Leadership
  Questionnaire (MLQ) 30, 116
Mumford, M.D. 102–3
music 11
Myth of Leadership, The
  (Nielsen) 56

Nanus, B. 18
narcissistic leaders 36–7, 102
  see also anti-narcissistic
     leaders
narrative analysis 94–5, 108
nature-nurture debate 16–17,
  23, 115
Neale, J. 27
needs 18, 54
Nelson, D.L. 59
new leadership 28–9, 31–2, 33
  see also charismatic leader-
     ship; transformational
     leadership
newspapers 4, 48
Nielsen, J. 56
normative control 93
North American contexts 69

observing leadership 5
on-the job leadership
    development 116–17
Open Road, The 38
organizational contexts 62
organizational culture and
    leadership 62, 64–7, 120
organizational performance
    101, 120
organizational politics 103
Orthwein, Peter 38
Osborn, R.N. 62
Osland, J.S. 74–5
Oswick, C. 108
outdoor challenge
    programmes 117

Palmer, I. 66
parent-child relationship
    50–1, 58–9, 98
    see also childhood experiences;
        families; parenting
parenting 16–17, 50, 105
Parry, K.W. 28, 30, 35, 66, 87,
    88, 89, 90–1, 102, 120
Passion for Excellence (Peters
    and Austin) 13
Pene, H. 80
People Express 48
Perceived Leader Integrity Scale
    (PLIS) 35
perceptions of leadership 75–8
personal power 19
personality 17–18, 23–4,
    34–6, 118
    see also narcissistic leaders
personality disorders 36
Peters, T. 13
Pfeifer, D. 78, 83–4
Pillai, R. 54–5
pilot studies 126
Podsakoff, P.M. 30, 31

poetry 107–8
political leadership 33, 34, 59,
    97–8, 102–3
Popper, M. 51
populist leaders 53
Porras, J.I. 37
Porter, L.W. 62
position power 19
Posner, P.Z. 31, 88, 89
post-charismatic leadership
    102–3
post-structuralist approaches,
    to followers 59–60
post-transformational
    leadership 102–3
power
    and dispersed leadership 90, 91
    and gender differences in
        leadership success 27
    personal and position 19
    power distance, as societal
        cultural dimension 71
    and pseudo-transformational
        leadership 99
    socialized power motivation 18
    see also control; empowerment
practices of leadership 89–90
pragmatic leadership 102–3
Prince, L. 80–1
Proctor-Thomson, S.B. 35,
    89, 120
professionals 45–6
programmes, leadership 10, 30,
    117, 122–3
projection 50, 51
prototypicality 52, 53, 54, 75
pseudo-transformational
    leadership 98, 99, 102
psychoanalytic theories of
    leadership 49–52
psychopaths 36
Pye, A. 28, 101, 106

qualitative methodologies 11,
    31, 32, 33
  see also case studies; discourse
    analysis; dramaturgical
    analysis; ethnography;
    humanities-based
    perspective; narrative
    analysis
quantitative methodologies 11
  see also empirical research;
    experimental studies;
    questionnaires
Queen, The 59
questionnaires
  cross-cultural leadership 70–2,
    74, 76–8
  feedback on leadership
    development 30, 116
  future research areas 120
  narcissistic leaders 37
  personality and leadership
    34–6
  romance of leadership 47
  team leadership 94
  transactional and
    transformational
    leadership 30–1, 32, 33
Quiet Leader, The
  (Badaracco) 38

Raelin, J. 56
RAMPP 89
reading about leadership 4, 5,
    126, 128, 147–8
reference books 147
reflection 123–4
relationship-oriented behaviour
    25, 26, 72
  see also affiliation, need for
religion 81, 100, 101
  see also spirituality of
    leadership; values
reputation 48

research questions 111
  see also future research areas
researching leadership
  context 84
  cultural influences 68–70
  versus developing
    leadership 113–14
  funding 114
  literature searching 126, 128
  methodology, choosing 125,
    127–8
  participants 126–7
  pilot studies 126
  research design, choosing 126
  research questions 111
  resources 114
  topic, choosing 124–5
  see also developing leadership;
    future research areas;
    methodologies; studying
    leadership
resilience 18
resources 113, 114, 119
  see also funding; time
Ritzer, D.R. 36
Romance of Leadership Scale
    (RLS) 47
romance of leadership theories
    47–9
Ropo, A. 109
Rosener, J.B. 104
Rost, J.C. 14–15

Schein, E.H. 64–5, 103
schooling, metaphor of
    leadership 105
Schwartz, S.H. 70–1, 74
Schyns, B. 8, 75
science, of sense-making 106
seduction 104
seeing leadership 5
selection, of leader, and identity
    theory of leadership 52–3

self-autonomous work
    groups 92
self-awareness 88, 122
self-concept 34, 101, 122
self-consciousness 88
Self Leadership 88
self-managed work teams 92–4
self-promotion, by managers 36
senior leaders 127
sense-making 28, 101, 106–8
servitude 42
Shackleton, Ernest 57–8, 62
Shamir, B. 34, 43, 50, 53, 54,
    60, 88, 94, 101
shared leadership 55–7, 83–4,
    94, 120
shared transformational
    leadership 85–8
Sims, H.P. 88
Sinclair, A. 123
Sinha, P. 89, 120
situational leadership 44–5, 62
situational validity 31–2
situations 62
    see also context; work
        environment
Smircich, L. 28, 101, 104
social capital 122
social construction 43, 48
social contagion 48
social identity theory of
    leadership 52–4
social network theory 94
social responsibility 103
societal cultural dimensions
    70–5, 76–8, 81
Sonnenfeld, J. 6
Sosik, J. 90–1
spirituality of leadership 100–2
Starratt, R.J. 111
status, as societal cultural
    dimension 71
Stech, E.L. 49, 50

Steidlmeier, P. 97, 98
stereotypes 52, 74, 104
Stogdill, R.M. 12–13
Storey, J. 9, 10–11, 102
Strodtbeck, F.L. 73
study, defined 3
studying leadership
    global reasons for 9–10
    internationalization 11, 12
    methods 3–6
    personal reasons for 6–8
    see also developing leadership;
        future research areas;
        researching leadership
'substitute of leadership' 45–6
SuperLeadership 88
support, for leaders 52–3, 54
Svejenova, S. 84, 87
Sveningsson, S. 56, 109–10

talking about leadership 3–4
Taoism 81
task-oriented behaviour 25, 26
    see also affiliation, need for;
        relationship-oriented
        behaviour
teaching leadership 115–16,
    117–19, 123–4
team leadership 94–5, 120
terrorist groups 96
Thomas, D. 67–8
Thompson, Wade 38
Thor Industries 38
time
    constraints in developing
        leadership 113, 114, 119
    constraints in researching
        leadership 126, 127
    present time as important for
        studying leadership 9–10
toxic leaders 51
training, formal, in developing
    leadership 117–19

traits 17–18, 23–4, 34–6, 118
transactional leadership
    29–31, 102–3
transference 50, 51
transformational leadership
    and authenticity 98–100
    communication styles 84
    described 28, 29
    and developing leadership
        119–20
    and followers 28–9, 30, 31, 44
    future research areas 32–3
    gender differences 25–6
    shared 85–8
    and spirituality of leadership
        100
    and transactional leadership
        29–31
    see also charismatic leadership;
        post-transformational
        leadership; pseudo-
        transformational
        leadership
    Transformational Leadership
        Questionnaire
        (TLQ) 30, 32
translation problems, in
    cross-cultural research 77–8
Triandis, H. 79
Trompenaars, F. 73–4
tyrants 97–8

Uhl-Bien, M. 54–5, 58
uncertainty avoidance, as societal
    cultural dimension 72, 74
unconscious processes 50–1,
    99, 115
Upper Echelons Theory 87

validity 31–2, 68–9
values
    and authentic and inauthentic
        leadership 98, 99

values cont.
    and cultural perspective on
        leadership 74, 75, 76–7,
        78, 79
    and humanities-based
        perspective 79
    and spiritual leadership 101
    and transformational
        leadership 98, 102
    see also ethical leadership;
        morality; religion;
        spirituality of leadership
Van Doorn, J. 102–3
Van Knippenberg, D. 52
Vine, B. 83–4
visionary leadership 36, 99
visual art 108

Waldman, D.A. 31
Ward, A, 6
Warner, L.S. 80
Watson, T.J. 128
Webster, S.W. 85
Weick, K.E. 28, 42, 106
Weldon, E. 68
Willmott, H. 89
wisdom 123, 124
wives 26, 27
women versus men as leaders
    25–8
    see also femininity; gender
work environment 26–7, 62, 120
writing about leadership 4–5, 128
    see also books; journals;
        newspapers

Yukl, G.A. 18, 19, 32, 116–17

Zaleznik, A. 18, 103